The Nepal Chronicles

THE NEPAL CHRONICLES

*Marriage,
Mountains, and Momos
in the Highest Place on Earth*

Dan Szczesny

Thanks for the support
Be Fearless!
Dan Szczesny

HOBBLEBUSH BOOKS
Brookline, New Hampshire

Composed in Janson Text at Hobblebush Books

Printed in the United States of America

Cover photograph by Meenakshi Gyawali
All other photographs by Dan Szczesny or Meenakshi Gyawali
Map illustration by Peter Noonan (www.noonanarts.com)

ISBN: 978-1939449-04-7
Library of Congress Control Number: 2014939330

HOBBLEBUSH BOOKS
17-A Old Milford Road
Brookline, New Hampshire 03033
www.hobblebush.com

Contents

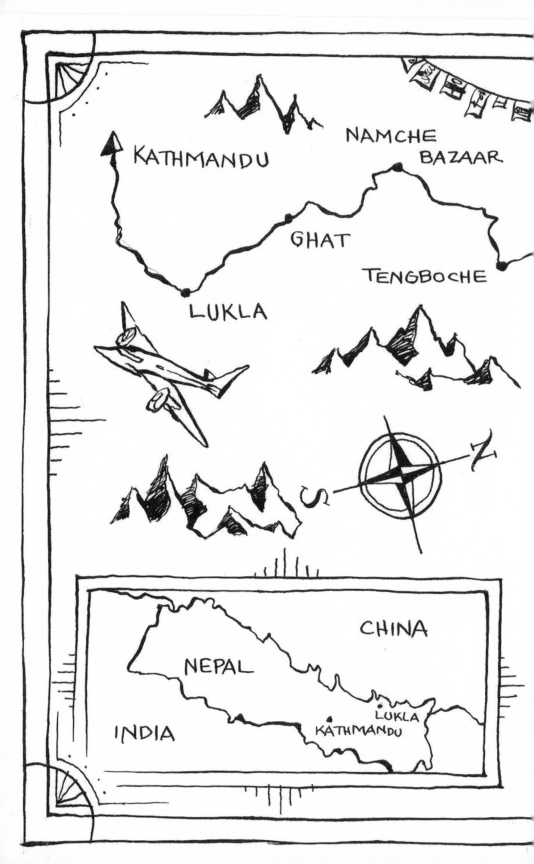

Acknowledgments

I'VE ALWAYS THOUGHT OF MY PATH AS ORGANIC. Around every turn is a new friend, or a new family, many of whom I never see coming. Looking back on this project—a project which is, in essence, my life—I am startled by how many people have helped and supported and eagerly embraced *The Nepal Chronicles*. And how many continue to do so. Thank you all!

To Rita and Kiran, for the speed at which you have welcomed me into your family, for the joy and kindness in your hearts and for never ceasing to amaze me with your ability to make me feel at home. Oh, and the mango lassi and goat curry as well!

To my new, amazing and extended family; they taught me, accepted me, encouraged me to write this book and now that I have, continue to treat me with love and support. You are too numerous to mention, but I am grateful to you all.

To my own family, for never doubting. Thanks Dad, Andrea, John, Ben and Max. Thanks Mom.

To my biggest fan, my alternate mom, Rita Slewinski, who has treated me like a son and whom I try every day to emulate.

To Sid Hall and Kirsty Walker at Hobblebush for having faith and sharing my passion for this project. And to my long-suffering editor, Lisa Parsons, who just rolls her eyes and gets to work every time a new manuscript drops into her in-box. To my friend and fine illustrator Peter Noonan who inspired the cover and created our map, for never saying no. And to Trish Herr for reading, and providing the kind blurbs.

To Lene Oh, Jim, Tim, Karen and every porter, guide, hiker, climber, trekker, shopkeeper, cook, lodge owner and friend we met along the way. There are too many to name. How I wish I could have told each and every one of your stories.

To Jeff DeRego and everyone in Spaghetti and Writers for always making it better.

To my dear friend and first reader, Margaret Bobalek King, for the encouragement and commitment that never waned, even when my own did.

To Janelle, my muse, and Aaron, my champion.

And finally, to Meenakshi. This is all for you.

To my Sasura Jyu and Sasu Jyu,
Kiran and Rita Gyawali

and to my father, Joseph

Introduction

WITH LESS THAN FORTY-EIGHT HOURS TO GO before my wedding, instead of celebrating my impending nuptials with my soon-to-be new family in Kathmandu, I was climbing the 268 steps to Tian Tan Buddha in Hong Kong.

We could have used a little serenity right about then, and one of the largest bronze Buddhas in the world seemed like the perfect place to shed the bad karma of the previous day, when, after twenty-four hours of flying to Nepal, we landed in Bangladesh instead.

We were only an hour from Kathmandu, but we might as well have been on the other side of the planet. And then, six hours later, our pilots flew us to Hong Kong.

Amid the chaos of trying to get another flight to Kathmandu in time for our wedding, we did manage to secure a room at the airport Marriott, along with vouchers for all the food we could eat for the next couple days. We stayed in Hong Kong for free, and slept and ate in a place we would never have been able to afford.

Meenakshi and I did make it out of Hong Kong the next day. And our visit to the Buddha was remarkable.

But it occurred to me later that so much of our relationship on the path to Nepal had been and continues to be about great reward preceded by great discomfort, that reaching that Buddha seemed an appropriate metaphor for everything we've ever done together.

You must climb those nearly 300 steps to get to that place of serenity and wisdom. We had to sit on that plane, eating peanuts and water, in order to make it to those stairs. We had to train for nearly a year, before getting on that series of flights that would eventually take us to Everest Base Camp. And before that, we climbed a mountain with a Justice of the Peace and sixteen bemused but willing friends in New Hampshire, our home state, on the day that a hurricane named Earl was visiting, to say "I do" from the top.

I met my wife years ago, when I was a lowly editor of a start-up newspaper and she was a city planner. For months, that paper ran story after story on city planning, all because the only thing I wanted to do once I met her was be near her.

Even then, every step forward in our relationship, in my courtship, was gained through sheer grit, or luck, or sacrifice. She is a native of Nepal. I was raised in Buffalo, New York. That might as well be the cultural equivalent of Mars and Venus.

She grew up in Chicago. I grew up in the suburbs. She had never been to Europe. I had never been to Asia. Her mind is a planner's, calculating, reasoned, deliberate. I am a writer.

But we forged a relationship out of two separate worlds by strapping backpacks to our shoulders and hitting the trail: the White Mountains, where we climbed all forty-eight of the state's highest peaks; the Dakotas, where we thru-hiked on the Centennial Trail, and the Grand Canyon, where we learned crucial lessons of patience and simplifying. By the time we decided to get married, it felt like we had nothing left to prove. We were not young. Our friends belonged to both of us. Our families appreciated us and loved us both.

But great discomfort to attain great reward came knocking again. Meenakshi's father asked if I would be interested in marrying his daughter in Kathmandu in a traditional Nepalese ceremony. I would be on my own. I'd need handlers to walk me through the traditions and tasks. I would be asked to abide by cultural mores for which I had no frame of reference and in some cases no understanding.

I said yes instantly.

Meenakshi and I upped the discomfort ante by deciding, for our honeymoon, to trek to Mt. Everest Base Camp and climb an 18,000-foot mountain called Kala Patthar for the sole reason of getting a better view of the tallest mountain on Earth.

Discomfort followed by reward. Only this time, on the biggest stage and grandest scale we could find.

So, that day, Meenakshi and I climbed those stairs and walked fully around the base of "The Big Buddha" passing by six smaller bronze statues known as the Offering of the Six Devas. These statues symbolize charity, morality, patience, zeal, meditation and wisdom.

In the days ahead—indeed throughout our lives—we would need to call on each of those Devas again and again. It wouldn't be easy. Sometimes, it wouldn't make sense.

But for all the challenge, for every moment where my legs betrayed me and the air felt like syrup in my lungs, and on the days when uncertainty clouded concentration, I knew—from experience and history—that the reward would always be great.

The lessons of our adventure are the same to anyone, on any journey great or small, and for any place. Put in the time. Say yes. And go with wonder in your heart. I hope you enjoy our journey, and I wish you many of your own.

Dan Szczesny
February 2014

The Nepal Chronicles

Prologue

To a westerner, Kathmandu speaks at one volume only, loud. But there's more to the city than the traffic and the people. Kathmandu rolls and boils and shouts in a cacophony all to itself: a symphony of chickens, goats and wild dogs; of bells around ankles and on bicycles and from temples; of the never-ending and unnerving static of motorbikes and the whiny hum of tuk-tuks; and of the sizzle and pop of roasted nuts and cart-side momos.

I allow myself to sink deeper into my barber chair and close my eyes as the boy works on my scalp. We don't understand each other anyway, so it is best to just give myself over to his attentions, come what may.

And slowly, as my hair comes off, so does my anxiety about this place. I begin to think that I can do this, I can walk among the chaos. Perhaps I won't understand it, but certainly I can accept it.

There appears to be no such thing as licensing here. The barber is also a masseuse, a stylist and a chiropractor. And since I had mentioned the name of my father-in-law, they were going to town on me. Once the hair is gone (a disconcerting feeling that takes me days to get used to) my head is thoroughly massaged and knocked about. He could be rubbing motor oil into my temples for all I know, but by the time he gets to the massage part of the proceedings I have stopped caring altogether and focus only on staying awake.

Outside the open-front barber stall, a happily clucking hen walks casually by, and I am happy as well.

The reason for the shave? Well, it does not take long in a place like Kathmandu to roll with the culture. Either that or sit terrified in your hotel room until the taxi comes to take you back to the airport.

After our wedding, we missed our flight out of Kathmandu to Lukla, the fascinating town that sits at nearly 10,000 feet and is the traditional starting point for most Nepal-side Everest treks. We missed the flight because weather on the mountain was not behaving.

In the West, when you miss your flight due to weather, the airline is quick to rebook you. In Kathmandu, when you miss a domestic flight, you simply go home. We had a set window for our trek, and after trying several avenues to rebook the flight we were at the end of our rope. Then, Meenakshi got angry.

We tracked down the booking agency, the one that originally chartered our flight. In Kathmandu, directions to a business often result in an Indiana Jones-like journey of discovery through back alleys and neighborhood squares. Our agency was a tiny storefront. One long counter. Three stools.

Without fanfare, Meenakshi announced to the startled proprietors that she was on her honeymoon and was not going to leave their establishment until we had been properly rebooked. Five minutes later, we had new tickets.

But would the weather be clear? Would the mountains allow us passage?

Meenakshi's father—a great philosopher if ever there was one— just shrugged at my anxiety. "Sometimes, you need to make a sacrifice," he said.

Of course! Not that I had much hair to give to the gods anyway, but by then I was ready and willing to take whatever steps might be necessary to get us on that plane. And with nearly 30,000 deities in Nepal, I didn't really even care which mountain god took heed of my offering.

The next day, we are on a plane and heading to the Himalayas. The flight is short, but long enough for me to consider the amazing path that had gotten us this far.

My wedding ride, a beautiful new Ford adorned with flowers, inches through Kathmandu traffic. In front of the car, a full-on wedding band is walking; the joyous group—a cross between Bollywood and an American marching band—is putting down some amazing licks. They are blowing hard and bystanders are beginning to notice.

We are a wedding procession. This little row of cars and musicians is taking me to our altar, to Meenakshi. This is *my* wedding procession. In Kathmandu.

As we pass, people stop and stare. A whole group of construction workers stops pouring cement and uses my passing to take a cigarette break. I wave and they wave back. They laugh in the universal way that all men do when they see another male on the way to his wedding.

Poor bastard. Lucky SOB.

A tiny, older woman in a dirty shawl moves close to my window to get a better look. I hold my ground and smile. Satisfied, she turns and continues on her way.

Kids on rusty, aching bikes peddle along, and motorbikers slow down as they pass.

Somewhere on the route, we pick up a tall western tourist with a video camera. Imagine how lucky he must feel, being able to bring back a videotape of an authentic Nepalese wedding procession. Oh, the stories he'll tell when he returns home, but I wonder if he even realizes I am a fellow westerner.

I suddenly feel like a fraud. Should I even be here? Is this the worst sort of cultural appropriation—me, here in a Nepali topi, or formal hat, given to me by my father-in-law along with the rest of my wedding clothes? Am I being sensitive enough and is that even possible given the amazing circumstances of a Polish boy from Buffalo in his own wedding procession in Kathmandu? My heart starts pounding and I begin to sweat.

I become so distracted by the internalization of my perhaps overly politically correct thoughts that I forget Meenakshi's grandmother is sitting next to me.

She is the elder here. She came from India to be with her granddaughter, whom she has not seen in years. She hadn't even met me until yesterday. She could decide to be anywhere she wanted. But instead of being with Meena waiting for me at the altar, she chose to drive with me. She chose to break who-knows-what tradition to sit in the back seat of the Ford with the nervous white boy who didn't speak Nepali. She chose to be here because, she said later, she didn't wish me to be alone.

And now, perhaps sensing my increasing discomfort, she reaches across the seat and takes hold of my hand, and squeezes. It is a gesture of such simple kindness that all I can do is say "thank you." She just smiles and nods, and I think to myself that maybe I'm going to be alright.

A couple years earlier, I attended the wedding of one of Meena's cousins in Massachusetts. Though being in an American reception hall is worlds away from being in Kathmandu, the traditions and symbols of the ceremony itself were similar to what I would now be going through.

At that wedding, Meena's dad stood next to me, quietly whispering in my ear the meaning of much of the ceremony as it was happening.

Now, as the car reaches the outdoor courtyard of the Russian restaurant where we are to marry, dozens of Meena's aunts swarm the parking lot, circling the car in dance and flinging marigold petals as a blessing and a greeting.

A traditional wedding can take a week or longer, but our condensed version will last two days. As I sit in the car and wait for the signal to leave, I watch, fascinated by the dancing women and men circling the auto. My father-in-law asked months ago if I wanted to ride to the wedding atop an elephant. I politely declined, but I have no idea if I was being teased or if I really could be sitting on an elephant right now.

We move into the stunning courtyard of the complex where the ceremony is to be held. My father and mother-in-law escort me to a seating area where I'm to await Meenakshi's arrival. I haven't seen her since she was whisked off in the morning. Meena was replaced by two English-speaking aunties from London who became my handlers for the day. They are my confidants and translators, giving me instructions and even helping me figure out how to tie the Daura-Suruwal, the traditional Nepali wedding suit that I am wearing, which requires a fair amount of tying and folding. They treat me with amazing patience and kindness, like a mother would treat a son getting ready to marry. I am a bit sad when they blend back into the crowd once I have been properly deposited into the high-backed red wedding chair.

Guests arrive and photographers and videographers swarm, wishing me well and taking pictures. I wave and nod as best I can.

Suddenly the cameras begin shooting over my shoulder and I know the bride has appeared. Meenakshi floats in like some sort of red and green sparkling apparition. Two young cousins walk in front, sprinkling rose petals, while several aunts jostle for primary position near the lady of the hour.

She is a waterfall of sequins and red and gold thread, starting from a small crown veil on her head, pouring down past her waist. With her face covered, she can barely see, thus the close attentions of her aunts.

The tradition of Nepali weddings is for the bride to keep her eyes downcast and be demure toward her guests and new husband. But as soon as my wife is deposited next to me, she turns and her eyes smile.

"You look spectacular," I say to her ear, likely breaking every rule in the books.

"I feel like a Christmas tree," she whispers, and we both laugh and the wedding is on.

While much of the Nepali wedding ceremony is based on Hindu tradition, my adoptive family has tossed in some western flair—the rose petals, for instance. We exchange rings during the ceremony as opposed to the night before.

An enormous amount of time is spent giving all the guests a chance to come and stand behind us for pictures. Everyone gets a chance, from the closest family to distant cousins, often with Meenakshi whispering in my ear who they each are. I wish I knew them better, that I had more history with them. Though that will certainly come later.

Unlike a typical western wedding ceremony, this one doesn't require guests to participate or even watch, and off to the side as our priest speaks to us in Sanskrit there is a dance competition going on among Meena's cousins. There are moments when even Meena needs to call out for someone to help with the translation.

There are offerings to the eight mountain Gods, including Everest (or Sagarmatha). That's a moment I try to pay close attention to given our plans for the very next day. There are games during the ceremony. During one, a coin is dropped into a big bowl of rice and Meena and I compete to fish it out. During another, there is a tug of war between cousins. Traditionally, these games are designed as ice-breakers because in arranged marriage situations, the two sides of the family may not know much about the other. There is a moment when I am escorted over an elaborately decorated stool by my father-in-law, a symbol of his welcoming me to his house.

My favorite moment is the tradition of moving Meenakshi from her house to mine, symbolized by my physically lifting her from her cushion to mine. And then my having to do it again because the photographer failed to get a picture the first time.

I move through these traditions not quite in a daze, but with something approaching ecstatic wonder. I try to be nonchalant, but fail terribly. Witnessing a Nepali wedding ceremony is one thing; it's something else entirely to be part of it. On one hand, I am completely entranced, fascinated and curious and eager to experience whatever peculiar custom comes next. On the other hand, I make a conscious effort to be aware that this day is peculiar only to me, and normal, perhaps even boring, to my new family.

And that I am lucky. Very lucky to be here at all.

Despite my attention, I don't realize until the end of the ceremony that the "I now pronounce you man and wife" part actually took place hours ago when we exchanged garlands. So now we're married.

Two months ago, we went to Buffalo to celebrate with my family. One month ago, we stood atop a mountain with a Justice of the Peace friend we call Farmer Bob and exchanged the words the state felt necessary. And today, we have been joined spiritually. In the days ahead, we will cement this series of "I dos" with our own personal quest for a mountain.

But today, we are the last in line for lunch at our own wedding ceremony. I have no shoes because part of the tradition is for

Meena's cousins to steal them and hold them hostage for money. My head and hands are coated thick with tika, the special rice paste used for blessings. Finally, on my wrist is tied a bright red slip of cloth, put there to symbolize my ties to this new family and new wife. It won't come off for months.

We are a couple. We are ready. There's just one more extraordinary obligation.

A couple hours later, at our reception, Meena and I stand alone outside the magnificent Hotel Shankar, guarding our gift basket.

The evening is warm and lovely and the elegant hotel grounds smell like summer grass and marigolds. We are in the heart of Kathmandu's residential neighborhood called Lazimpat, surrounded by hotels, restaurants and homes. The neoclassical Shankar is lit pure white, glowing in the night like an ice castle. I imagine you can see it from space.

Our guests and friends and family are enjoying our reception, and from the hotel grounds where we wait, we can hear the faint strains of Bollywood music. The electro thump of the popular Bollywood song "Desi Girl" crashes out into the night and I lean back on the bench and breathe in this night.

We ought to be in there, of course, and just a few moments ago we were. But we decided to take a walk out on the grounds and that's when we noticed our reception basket that contained all the kind gift envelopes from our guests was sitting on a table in the middle of the Shankar's garden. Somewhere in the barely controlled madness of the evening, when everyone was herded into the hotel from the grounds outside, the basket was left.

And now we're trying to figure out what to do with it.

"Well, Desi Girl," I say to Meena, "sounds like they're having fun in there."

She smiles. "Wait here, let me find my mother."

I sneak a kiss and watch her leave, marveling at the stunning reception sari she changed into after the ceremony. The glow of the hotel spotlights refracts off her sequins and as she moves the dress seems to spin like a brilliant red disco ball.

I'm alone now. I lean back and close my eyes, trying to remember a moment in my life when I was happier. I am startled by the time and effort that Meenakshi's parents put into creating this wedding for us. It feels like a fairy tale here outside this amazing complex.

In a city this ancient, the Shankar is relatively young, built in 1894 not for royalty but for a general. General Jit Shumsher hired one of the first civil engineers in Nepal, Kumar Narsingh, to construct the palace in European style and it stayed in the family until 1964.

Now, as a gleaming, modern hotel, the Shankar has seen its fair share of celebrities, including the most famous Sherpa in the world, and a fellow whose footsteps we'll literally be following toward Everest tomorrow: Tenzing Norgay, who along with Edmund Hillary was one of the first people to reach the top of Everest, frequently stayed at the Shankar.

Meena finally returns with someone from the staff who takes our basket for safekeeping.

"Guess we need to dance," she says.

In the morning, we will begin the long, complicated journey to Mt. Everest and toward our own mountain, Kala Patthar. But tonight, we need to dance.

I take her hand and the two of us walk back to the reception hall, where the music booms and a fog machine has begun to push mist onto the golden dance floor. Tonight, we have a cake to cut. Tomorrow, we set out for the Himalayas.

Chapter 1
—
Airport in the Clouds

THE TWIN OTTER AIRPLANE pitches hard right, then levels off, and I peek out my dirty, scratched window to see a farmer digging in the soil near his stone home. The farmer is so close I can see the tears in his thin, fur-lined shawl. I check my altimeter: 9,900 feet.

The noise in the Lukla-bound plane is fierce, even through the cotton I stuffed in my ears thirty minutes ago as we sat on the tarmac in Kathmandu waiting for the copilot to eat a warm lunch.

"I'm not going anywhere without a warm lunch," Meenakshi translated. So we sat there until his food was brought out to the cockpit, where he leaned back in his chair and took his time eating.

The copilot is young, late 20s maybe, wearing a crisp white shirt over perfectly creased dress pants and shined black shoes. His hair is dark and wavy. He wears Ray-Bans, of course.

The domestic pilots of Nepal are legendary. Like the bush pilots of Alaska, they fly old, beat-up planes over some of the most demanding terrain and weather in the world. Mostly, they do this without radar, by sight. There's a saying among Nepali pilots that goes something like this: "Never fly into a cloud, because you don't know what might be in there."

They are, more or less, the only thing that works about domestic air travel in Nepal.

Tribhuvan International Airport in Kathmandu certainly does not work. There's nothing that can prepare a Westerner for the mad chaos of the domestic terminal of Kathmandu's only airport—there appears to be virtually no order, certainly no lines and even less system. Getting on your plane is like winning the lottery. Perhaps it's no small irony that the airport is named after King Tribhuvan—who became king in 1911 at the prime-time age of five years old. Unlike the airport named after him, however, Tribhuvan was organized and ambitious, taking on the country's powerful prime minister through his plan of an elaborate self-exile to India and finally returning in full control of the monarchy in the 1950s. He died mysteriously in Switzerland in 1955 and his son's naming the airport after him may have been the last logical thing that ever happened to the place—both the airport, and perhaps, the country.

Still, if you somehow manage to make it to your flight, if you are able to get on board—through a guide, with a porter, by way of bribery or, as we managed it, by dint of sheer aggressive behavior—you're in good hands.

But that's cold comfort as the plane skims the green and brown ridge tops and somebody from the back whispers, "Look, look." I have to half-stand in my seat to see through the open cockpit door and out the pilots' window to glimpse the thin asphalt strip of the Lukla runway. It seems impossible to imagine an airport in this place—wind, mist, clouds, rain and snow are more common than not up here and any one of those things can close the airport for days.

This is Hillary's fault, really, all this traffic and the asphalt. A few years ago, Edmund Hillary, the first European to scale Mt. Everest, had the runway built, and that opened up the Khumbu in a way no one could have imagined. In 2008, the airport was christened the Tenzing-Hillary Airport, partly after the famous Brit, but mostly after Tenzing Norgay, the Nepali-Indian Sherpa who is equally, if not more, famous in this region of Nepal, the Khumbu, as his western partner.

Now, nothing short of half a dozen local airlines ply this tiny bit of pavement on the side of a mountain, and thousands of tourists, scientists and trekkers every year brave the Lukla flight to get an advanced leg up on the trail to Everest. If you don't want to risk the flight, you start your trek a week earlier, because you need to walk five days from distant Jiri, the city with the nearest bus stop.

Still, the runway is less than 500 meters long and requires a 12-percent grade to help planes stop when they come in, and give them an extra bit of push on the way out.

I swallow hard and sit back down.

"Whoa," Meenakshi murmurs. She's sitting directly behind me—single seats on the left side.

"Almost there," I say and smile weakly, out of nerves and the fact that I'm still coming off a flu-like bug that laid me out for most of yesterday. Allergy to Kathmandu and its foul air perhaps? Either way, Meenakski's auntie plied me with hot water treatments and vaporizers until the bug was reduced to the dull, sweaty headache I am now dealing with. Add altitude into the mix and a two-day delay getting a plane ride to Lukla, and I'm ready to start walking.

The plane dips hard, and the copilot adjusts the friction control, casually joking with the pilot as the plane screams toward the tiny runway. There are no second chances in Lukla. Come in too low and the Twin Otter becomes a burst of squashed metal on the head of a 2,000-foot cliff. Take too long to touch down, and a concrete and stone retaining wall at the end of the runway will bring the plane to a quick end. One shot is all you get.

But even as the fifteen or so passengers aboard the small plane collectively gasp as the worn tires touch down, the pilots think nothing of it. They calmly throw down the flaps and reverse the props in a cloud of dust and I feel the pull on my seat belt. The runway's incline helps the plane stop well before the flight-ending wall, and just like that we are on the side of a mountain about thirty miles of hard walking away from Mt. Everest.

A few of us applaud, one supposes for a job well done by the pilots, but mostly because we're all so damned relieved to finally be here. Once the plane taxis to the basketball-court-sized terminal parking area, all they want to do is get us out. Good weather is so rare up here that the airlines fly like heck to get tourists back and forth. The way to land is the same flight path as the way to take off, and the turnaround time for getting planes back in the air is only about fifteen minutes.

So off we go, hustled onto the tarmac where vaguely official-looking men half guide us toward . . . what? A chain link fence surrounds the airstrip, behind which swarm literally hundreds of would-be porters and Sherpas looking for work. It's been three days since planes landed in Lukla—planes carrying people like me who will hire these scruffy-looking fellows to do one of two things, either carry your gear or guide you where you wish to go. Here, like everywhere else in the world, jobs are scarce, and a three-day backup of men has accumulated in Lukla, just waiting for the planes to start arriving.

They are a mixed lot at best, most fairly desperate-looking, hanging on the fence, two and three deep, watching for any eye contact that might indicate my desire to find a hired hand.

But of course, we're carrying our own packs and we're guiding ourselves.

A word on the hierarchy of Khumbu trekking. There are those who trek in a group with an organization that hires the porters and Sherpa. There are those who trek in a group without any organization, who hire their own porters and Sherpa. There are those who trek in ones or twos who hire, perhaps one porter. And then there is us. We are in the minority, as it turns out. In the pecking order of this region, we will eventually earn grudging respect from the Sherpas for hauling our own gear, for taking this journey without porter support . . . eventually, but not now.

A small opening in the gate appears and we are shuffled into the tiny concrete baggage area to await arrival of our luggage. The room is basically a brown box, with one door and one window facing the tarmac. One guy throws the luggage through the window to a second guy waiting outside. When your baggage gets through the window, you point frantically and shout at the guy until he notices, then you politely show him your luggage tag. Like everything else in Nepal, it's a system that on paper could not possibly work. But it does.

Dozens of porters looking for work have poured into the cramped room behind us. Meena skitters off to find a bathroom, while I fend off a half dozen porters. "Carry, carry?" they ask. Some hold slips of paper that explain their fees or simply have destinations scribbled down: Namche, Tengboche, for example, an indication of how far they are willing to trek with you.

I wave them off as best I can, but they are persistent, and when my backpack does arrive I practically have to push them away, so eager are they to grab my pack and start walking.

Meenakshi arrives and parts the boys with a few choice words in their native language. The pack slinks off, leaving us alone. Meena's hands are still deep burnt red with wedding henna and many of the porters don't know what to make of a Nepali Brahmin woman, newly married, trekking in the Khumbu and carrying her own gear. And with a white boy! Later we'll discover our odd-couple situation will become both an advantage and a handicap for us.

For now, we're free to go, so we shoulder our loads and finally, after days of uncertainty, we're on the trail and heading to Everest.

Imagine our surprise when one of the first buildings we come across, just outside the airport, shining like a freakish but comfortable beacon, is a Starbucks.

Chapter 2

—

Valley of Firsts

Lukla boils over, a rolling cauldron of impatient sound and fury.

To a Westerner, even one who has spent the last week and a half navigating the chaos of Kathmandu, Lukla is daunting.

Where Kathmandu is crowded, loud, and sometimes dirty, Lukla is all those things condensed into a five-block space, but mostly it is rowdy.

It is the ultimate truck stop, a juke joint at the end of the world, the Wild West with yaks.

Lukla is a town for porters and Sherpas looking for work. It is where the men bring their children and wives and mistresses, and they are all outside, running and shouting and playing games.

Three days have passed since a plane landed in Lukla, three days with no supplies, no trekkers and no work. And the residents are letting out some steam.

Even before we pass the fake Starbucks, the "Scottist" and Irish pubs and the disco lounge, a small child, maybe seven years old, with mud on his face and a huge grin, tears out of a dilapidated building and runs straight for me, yelling. Before I can do or say anything, the boy throws his arms around my legs, like I'm a long-lost uncle. I pat his head and look to Meena for guidance, but of course she just laughs.

The boy runs off and I instinctively check my pockets, but feel guilty doing it. In Rome I was pickpocketed in a similar manner, but here, perhaps the boy was just happy to see a Westerner.

The moment is a mystery, one of many I'll face in the next two weeks.

We hustle through the nightlife section of town. The Starbucks is not real. Instead of a mermaid, the Lukla Starbucks logo has an image of Ama Dablam mountain. We decide not to stop, though this mock Starbucks will play a role in our journey fourteen days later.

The main street is a cacophony of sights and sounds. Children scream and shout and laugh, literally everywhere. They play in the dust and dirty stream, they toss stuffed animals about and roll marbles. They squat on the stone ledges and hang from railings and huddle in dark doorways.

We are the first sure sign that the planes are flying again, and some kids, and adults, see us and hurry by toward the airport and perhaps a job. Most, though, don't much seem to care.

Today is a warm day, the skies are mostly clear and everyone is outside. A crowd of men playing ping-pong on a bruised piece of plywood smash the plastic ball at each other. Elsewhere, a scene that will be repeated time and time again on our journey: several men surround a low table, covered with talcum power. They are playing carrom, sort of like pool, only players use their fingers to shoot disks into corner pockets. The talcum smooths the worn pieces of wood or old boards that the village players have constructed for the game, and the players appear to be surrounded in a cloud of white dust. Carrom is popular on the Indian subcontinent but reaches out to Central Asia and the Middle East as well. Like soccer, it can be played with minimal equipment, anywhere, and with built boards.

There are no women playing these games. They don't have the time. While the men wait for work, the women run lodges, restaurants, and their homes. Walk past a terraced garden or a field being worked, and invariably it is the women doing those jobs.

We're tired from the morning's wait at the airport, and hungry, but eager to get out of town and into the valley, away from Lukla.

As so often is the case with Nepal, a trekker is faced with a paradox at the start of any trip to Everest—a memorial gate, offering words of encouragement and welcome. The brightly colored arch used to read "Have your nice trek" but someone has blotted out most of the "your" and replaced it with the more correct "a."

Just getting this far is a huge achievement for us. This is the official start of the trek, and our spirits are lifted by the sight of this gate, which to me has come to represent the beginning of a great adventure.

But Nepal is not an easy country. Success is often offered in only somber tones.

The National Luminary Pasang Lhamu Memorial Gate is dedicated to a national hero in Nepal. In 1993, Pasang Lhamu was the first Sherpa woman to attain the summit of Mt. Everest. For this achievement, she was granted the title of National Luminary, a sort of knighthood in Nepal.

But Pasang Lhamu died on the descent, while attempting to save the life of a team member on the South Summit. And so here we were, celebrating the beginning of our journey while also remembering her tragedy. The Khumbu is like that.

We move into the valley at an easy pace. The trail to Everest starts slow and flat and winds down toward the river. The valley walls shoot straight up around us, thousands of feet, rising in fertile waves. Far below, the Dudh Koshi, or Milk River, roars, pouring mightily down from the glaciers.

In a short time we leave the noise of Lukla behind and wander contently through terraced farmland dotted with stone Sherpa homes. Their stone animal pens look surprisingly like New England stone walls.

The day is bright, though clouds linger at the ridge tops, and the comforting weight of my pack on my hips relaxes my mind. The Khumbu! I'm on the ground, feet pointed toward the top of the world; my new bride walks by my side. There are few moments in life as exhilarating as the opening steps of a long trek.

Our day of firsts takes us through the tiny village of Chheplung, a modest collection of lodges and homes, and over our first suspension bridge—a worthy picture opportunity for any trekker.

Though the days of twisting rope bridges are long gone on the well-trekked parts of the country, the metal frame structures still require something of a leap of faith to cross. And timing.

Fail to get across before the yaks step on from the other side, and you've no choice but to turn around and go back.

Rule Number One of Nepal trekking: Yaks always get the right of way.

A yak train is on the bridge as we approach and we get out of the way quickly to let them pass. The beasts are the semi-trucks of the Everest region, carrying everything from food to lodge supplies to trekkers' gear.

Technically, down here in the lower altitudes, the animals that pass us are dzopkyos, a crossbreed between cows and yaks. No matter. They are giants, and it's clear that a careless trekker is one misguided horn or head push away from being over the bridge rail without even realizing what has happened. For the next two weeks we use the mellow jingle of yak bells on the trail as an excuse to take a break.

After the bridge, the trail hugs the folds in the valley, and we suddenly come upon an enormous mani stone. It's fascinating art, intricately carved with Tibetan symbols, and two stories high.

The stone is a reminder that this trail—unlike a maintained trail in the White Mountains, for example—is also a road, a pilgrimage path and a holy place to the people of the region. Mani stones and prayer wheels are everywhere, a constant companion and testament to the spiritual dedication of Nepali and Tibetan Buddhists.

The stones are carved primarily with the mantra "Om Mani Padme Hum." The Sanskrit and Tibetan forms vary slightly, as do the Bodhisattvas to whom the mantra is directed, but the phrase is generally recognized to mean "Behold! The jewel in the lotus!" But then again, it doesn't mean that either.

The meanings can be very confusing. But it also doesn't matter.

Before the trip, Meenakshi suggested that there would be things I saw that would not make sense to me, that the best way to understand and not be overcome by culture shock would be to simply box the things I didn't understand in a part of my mind for later reference.

And so, as we came upon this beautiful carving, reflecting brilliantly in the sun, I did just that. And now, in retrospect, I still don't understand the history, but I think I understand the meaning. I found a fable about understanding the mantra, which I'll paraphrase:

A devoted meditator had spent years learning the correct form and pronunciation of the mantra. After some years of teaching, he learned of an old hermit on an island, so he rented a boat and went to visit the hermit. He was pleased to learn the hermit used the same mantra as he, but horrified that the hermit, for all his life, had been pronouncing the mantra incorrectly! He immediately corrected the hermit and taught him the proper pronunciation.

In the boat on the way back to the mainland, the meditator felt sorry for the hermit that he had spent his whole life saying the mantra wrong. Suddenly, he turned to see the hermit walking on the water to catch up to the boat. The shocked meditator waited while the hermit came up to the floating boat and said, "I'm sorry to bother you, but I've forgotten the correct pronunciation. Would you please repeat it for me?"

And I say Om Mani Padme Hum, baby! Om Mani Padme Hum.

After the Mani, the valley opens and we descend into Ghat, a small farming village at the bottom of a col in the trail, the low point between two hills. Above the village to the north is a ridge and further along is Phakding, a larger town, clearly identified and suggested in the tour books as the place to bed down on day one.

But I'm tired from my recent flu and we stop for a snack of bread and cheese at a tiny roadside lodge where the air is still and warm. The river rushes by a hundred yards off the trail. There are no tourists, and no lights. There is a towering peak across the valley and the afternoon sun has lit the top on fire. That mountain is a beacon, and we both know it.

Two young boys, maybe eleven or twelve, take turns serving us and I follow one inside to ask about lodging. The place is called the Himalayan Sherpa Lodge and it's warm, and cozy, and a single Sherpa woman has begun stocking the kitchen's single stove with wood, the long sticks protruding out the opening near the floor. The kitchen smells like cabbage and alu, or potatoes.

A room is 200 rupees, about $3, and it's clean and bright and faces a grassy courtyard out back where a group of porters have erected a set of tents. Their clients will be staying inside at the lodge next door. The porters, however, huddle outside around a giant pot, making soup for themselves perhaps, while they await their clients. I watch the scene for a bit, feeling very happy.

"It's perfect," I announce to Meenakshi coming back down, where she sits at an outside table facing the trail. "It will be quiet here and all the tour groups are going to Phakding, and staying here will only add about twenty minutes to our day tomorrow."

But she's deep into a cup of lemon tea, and she offers me a stick of yak cheese, which is so delicious I almost start to cry, and I realize that even though it's only four in the afternoon I don't have to talk her into staying here tonight.

We are on our own, on our own schedule. We have no agenda except to walk or not as we please, and so we stay, and we eat our Tibetan flat bread and watch the groups go rushing by, sometimes not even picking up their heads long enough to say hello even though we are only feet from the road.

A huge tribe of gray and white goats comes floating by, like hairy little apparitions.

With some time to spare before dinner, we stroll down behind the lodge, down a small embankment used, it seems, only for locals, and to the river's edge where we cross a rickety wooden bridge and go down to the river.

Even in October the Milk River rages, the rapids bright white and foaming. The surge must be incredible in the springtime!

I step to the river and reach my bare hand into the water. The headwaters of the Dudh Koshi come from the Ngozumpa Glacier, one of the largest in the world, and only about twenty miles away. As the river roars into our valley, it is joined by two smaller rivers, the Imja and the Lobuche. Those three waterways pour down from the Khumbu Glacier, Everest's glacier. I feel giddy, and a bit silly, thinking that I'm touching Everest's water, down here in this tiny farming town, in a lush valley, waiting for my dinner, on the first day of the trek.

As night falls, we return to our lodge, feeling relaxed and content. We pass a couple checking their maps on the way to Phakding. With heavy packs on their backs and no tour group in sight, it's clear they are one of us.

Tim and Karen, a Canadian and New Yorker, are solo trekking as well. They've been on the road for months, hopscotching around the world and now, like us, they are heading to Everest.

We chat a while, suggest they might like Ghat, and leave them, fresh and happy and excited like us. We don't know it then, but the two would later become close friends and important trekking partners.

We return to the lodge as the sun sets, and sit outside sipping tea for as long as we can. We are the only guests at the lodge and our hostess is making dinner for us, her two boys helping in the kitchen.

There is electricity in the village but it's spotty and often goes out. The kitchen fire and headlamps of passing trekkers then become the only light.

The dinner is simple, vegetables mostly, and it takes a long time, but we are impatient Westerners. We learn on this first night, that evenings are for conversation and dinner should be ordered several hours before you are actually hungry.

The lodge is typical. The seating area is a square, with long tables around the edges for guests and cushions on the seats to double as sleeping cots for porters, or trekkers if the rooms are all booked. This is a design that repeats itself over and over with some variations all though the Khumbu.

It turns out our host is running the lodge while her husband is off working, earning a living as a guide. While the word Sherpa has come to mean a porter to the west, the Sherpa people nowadays are mostly guides or high altitude climbers, while porters come from the Kathmandu Valley or even further away, in some cases as far away as India or Pakistan, looking for work.

This week is Dashain and one of her sons is home for the holidays. We learn that he has found a western sponsor who has helped send him to school in Kathmandu.

This is a huge score, and something that families in the mountain region dream about and sometimes actively pursue. While an education in Kathmandu is not possible for the children of most Sherpa families, to Westerners, the cost is negligible. Our hostess is very lucky.

Our food arrives, after an hour and a half, and our stomachs are rumbling, but the wait is worth it. Fresh from the earth behind the lodge, we eat a spring roll the size of a calzone, the carrots tasting as sweet as candy. We have a plate of heaping noodles, with onions and cabbage, and a dish of rice and dahl so large we are unable to finish the helping, and our hostess scolds us for leaving rice on our plate. We top off the dinner with a tremendous salad, the lettuce so crisp the crunch is deafening and tomatoes so juicy, red streaks pour down our cheeks. We struggle to eat every last bite of the salad as we don't wish to displease our hostess again.

Our stomachs full, our hostess happy, the boys washing dishes, our heads swimming from our first day on the trail, we retire to our simple, plywood room.

Outside, the porters are all in their tents, the lights of the town have once again gone out and somewhere in the distance a single yak is ringing his bell softly like a lullaby.

Sleep is easy that night, and morning takes a long time to arrive.

Chapter 3

~

Into Thinnish Air

I wake but think I'm dreaming.

There's gentle music playing, and in those few moments of early rising, it sounds like someone is singing Om Mani Padme Hum. It's a pleasant dream, though a bit typically Western considering the day I had yesterday.

After a few minutes, I realize that I am actually awake, and someone is actually singing this to me. Certainly not Meenakshi, whose head is still buried deep in her sleeping bag.

Woozily, I get up. It's six a.m. and the sun has just begun to fire up the ridge tops.

Outside, somewhere, someone is playing a record and the sound is echoing through Ghat, bouncing off the valley walls.

"Om Mani Padme Hum." Over and over, the chant churns. It's a tremendous way to wake up, as soft and mellow as a lazy summer afternoon.

I put down the cynical thoughts that crop up, that some village elder with an eye and ear toward making Western tourists happy is looking to loosen our valuable dollars in his town. That may be the case, but it is still one of the best wake-up calls I will experience on the trip.

This is going to be a longer day today than we had originally planned, so we settle on a quick breakfast of Tibetan bread with melted yak cheese and milk tea.

Soon, we are back on the trail, moving up a slight slope out of town. We pass through a series of mani stones and prayer wheel chapels. On one three-foot prayer wheel in the center of a small square is a note from Llama Dorgee that reads "Please, turn round this (mani) thrice. You get rid of sin. You can obtain religion and the period of life. Please take part and use up." I spin the wheel thrice, taking part and hopefully obtaining the aforementioned period of life.

The path climbs a steep rise and tops out with a wonderful view down toward the Milk River, and we can see the trail hook around the valley wall and disappear out of sight some miles away. At the top of this rise, painted onto a flat, knee-high stone is the message that we are two hours away from the monastery. Perhaps that refers to the hundred-year-old Tibetan Buddhist Monastery in Tengboche, located well beyond Namche Bazaar. Clearly, the sign is for Sherpa locals and porters, as it would be impossible for us to reach it in two hours. From this point, it will take us nearly six more hours just to reach Namche, our destination for the day.

We drop down toward the river again and, thinking ahead to our hike back, Meenakshi jokes that the trail to Everest is uphill both ways. Indeed, over the course of the next week, the trail will dip wildly up and down the valleys and we'll spend many days losing elevation gained the day before, only to have to climb back up again.

We swing around a ridge near the floor of the valley and climb up to the village of Phakding. This was to be our original destination the night before, and the town is obviously a popular place. Just outside the village is an enormous lodge, very new, with all the amenities. It looks more like a resort. In town there is a Jamaican Reggae bar, pool halls and trekking gear shops.

It's loud. There are tight groups of Western trekkers in every corner, pulling gear together or waiting for porters to begin their day. We don't stay long, and we are happy we picked our little village lodge for our first night's rest.

We cross another suspension bridge and walk through the grounds of the Sunrise Lodge on the west side of the river. It's not quite fall yet in the Khumbu and the Sunrise is awash in vibrant orange and red flowers, hundreds of marigolds flooding the courtyard and garden. We stop for a quick cup of lemon tea and enjoy the color and the sun.

We don't know it yet, but it's the last we'll see of sun and blue skies for the next three days.

We wind along the west side of the river, past the amusingly named village of Toc Toc and next to a beautiful triple-layered waterfall, at the base of which locals are washing clothes.

The valley narrows into a wash of rhododendron bushes and pine and begins to resemble a Swiss landscape, with short but steep steps up and down over little bumps, with the top of each steep pull offering a better view then the last.

Finally, after passing through the village of Benkar, we come upon a mountain. The very top of it is lost in a fog that will eventually swallow us for the next several days. Its icy flanks seem to shoot straight up above a perfect V in the valley walls.

This is the southern ridge of Thamserku, a 21,729-foot mountain that rises to the east of Namche. It's shrouded in mist. Even though the ridge we can see is not the summit, I stop to catch my breath. I stand at the edge of the path and stare at the glistening ice that looks like white aluminum foil rising up to a razor ridge.

I've never seen a 20,000-foot mountain before. At this moment, I have no idea what mountain I am looking at, only that we are going there. I swallow hard, put my head down and move on.

The trail moves across the river once more and jags into a small inlet. We lose sight of the valley. It's here that I finally become aware of our altitude. A long sharp incline of 150 feet or so swings us around the valley ridge, and I am suddenly out of breath. My altimeter reads less than 10,000 feet. I slow my pace and before long my lungs are back to normal, but it's a foreshadowing of what's to come.

Near Monjo, we encounter a resting trekking group and I'm thrilled to discover our friend Jim is one of the team. We exchange hugs and high fives. Gregarious and upbeat, our Canadian friend is part of a team raising awareness of multiple sclerosis—Jim's wife suffers from the disease and he has dedicated his recreation time to trekking to raise money for a cure.

Though we're friends through Facebook and his website, we met Jim for the first time only a few days ago at his hotel in Kathmandu. He explains that, like ours, his team's plane had been grounded, but his guide managed to find them helicopter transport to Lukla. Still, they are a couple days behind and moving fast and hard to reach their goals.

The four-day back-up in Lukla has created a vicious domino

effect in the Khumbu, an effect we see and feel through the whole trek—porters pushing their Western teams particularly hard to make up time. The result is often sick and discouraged trekkers leaving their breakfasts on the side of the trail or having to be horse-carried back down because of altitude sickness.

It's hard to not like Jim, and I feel a kinship given that I followed his training and struggles online as he, too, prepared for this journey. That said, I am concerned about the schedule that his group is now forced to follow.

"Have you seen Namche?" he asks with a smile.

"What do you mean?"

Jim points up valley. And there it is.

The Namche Bazaar plateau rises up before us, a brown mound 11,300 feet above sea level. Directly above it soars the perfect gray and white triangle of the guardian mountain of the Khumbu, Khumbi Yul Lha.

The 20,000-foot mountain is sacred to the Sherpa people, a "personality" mountain, according to tradition. It rises up at the split in the valley. At the mountain's foot the Milk River continues to the east, toward Everest, while the Bhote Koshi ("Bhote" is a Nepali term that roughly means Tibet or refers to Tibetan people) splits off and heads west.

So holy is the mountain that the Nepalese government does not allow it to be climbed and does not issue permits.

Khumbi Yul Lha is a warrior divinity. The white ice and snow embody the warrior's benevolence while the gray represents strength. The mountain is worshiped in Namche every morning with prayer and juniper incense.

We bid farewell to Jim and his crew and hurry off toward the Sagarmatha National Park entrance, where we check in. With some difficulty we bought our trekking pass in Kathmandu thinking it would save us time and energy here. We were wrong. The agents at the National Park are far more efficient and courteous than anyone we encountered in the city. Another tip of the trek: The Khumbu is more functional than Kathmandu.

Built in a small col at a split in the valley above the river, the park headquarters is a new, beautiful, modern building with a museum and topographical maps. A company of the Nepal Army is there as well, ostensibly to protect the park, but the question of what they actually do is a real one.

In fact, despite having been formed in 1976, the viability of the park itself is a topic of great conversation among locals in the Khumbu.

The main reason for the park's existence is environmental protection. The onset of trekkers in the last few decades led to massive stripping of the region's forests for lumber to build the lodges and restaurants that cater to tourists. Now, no wood is allowed to be cut in the park.

But that's a lot of land now off limits to the locals—more than 1,100 kilometers, 30 percent of which is grazing land or forest. The result has been immediate. Locals now have to use yak dung or dead wood to stoke their fires, and the establishment of the park has created something of an "us against them" attitude among the Khumbu leaders.

At a cost of 500 rupees for a park permit, there's a lot of money that should be going into the Khumbu. But it doesn't.

The trails are maintained by locals, who occasionally even reach out to trekkers for help with path maintenance. In large towns like Namche and Loboche, research centers and hydro parks are built by outside governments.

In recent years, the army stationed in the park has done little other than checking tourist permits. During our entire trek, we never saw a single officer on the trail or in any of the villages.

Even rescue missions are paid for by the trekker needing the rescue. Stories abound in the Khumbu of sick trekkers having to pull out a credit card on the spot and pay the several thousand dollars before the helicopter pilot would even let them on the bird.

So where does the money go? No one knows, though many have theories, mostly revolving around government corruption.

"They do nothing," said one lodge owner who said he'd been to Kathmandu to try to petition the state to better fund the national park. "They sit in their office with their feet up and read the newspaper."

We walk through the colorfully adorned Kani Gate, an entryway designed to ward off any evil spirits that might consider attaching to an unwary traveler, and drop sharply into the valley, losing hundreds of hard-gained feet from earlier that day.

On all sides of us, massive valley walls shoot straight up from the river, and thousand-foot waterfalls cascade down the rock. The stone path leads to yet another suspension bridge and we trot into the final village before Namche.

It's past midday now and we stop for a plate of momos and fried rice at the first clean lodge we see. Once again we are reminded that meals are not fast in this part of the world. The food sets us back a half hour more than we'd like, but soon we are again crossing a suspension bridge and find ourselves at water's edge.

From here it's a half mile of beautiful river walking to the split in the valley that will lead us to Namche.

There are seven rivers that form this river system in eastern Nepal, all of them draining down from Everest's massif. It's a harsh and fast-moving system, burning white foam crashing over round boulders at unimaginable speeds, particularly in the spring.

The Milk River itself was not kayaked until 1976. A British expedition, led by white-water rafter Mike Jones, estimated that the water in some sections of the river fell at a rate of more than 250 feet per mile, about fifty miles per hour. Jones wrote a book, *Canoeing Down Everest*, and made a movie of the expedition, now a classic in extreme sports films. Two years later, Jones died on the Braldu River in Pakistan while trying to save a teammate. His bravery earned him England's Queen's Gallantry Medal.

It's a magical place, this stretch of the trail. The roar of the river is the white noise behind the constant jangle of yak bells, and amid the feeling of truly entering the mountains. From the river bed, the valley walls rise unrelentingly and a fine fog hangs thousands of feet above our heads, beckoning us to climb into it like a London night.

At around two p.m., at an elevation of about 9,300 feet, Namche's plateau finely comes into view. We stop on a small bluff and stare down at the enormous plain that soaks up the rushing water from two of the Khumbu's rivers.

At the head of the plain, rising more than two thousand feet into the clouds, is a triangular block of rock and forest. Our trail makes a sharp right turn here and ascends several hundred feet up the eastern valley wall, then cuts left to a very high suspension bridge that appears to disappear into a sheer wall of green on the other side. It's high, and the wind blows the shredded prayer flags on the bridge. We know our work is cut out for us.

There's a traffic jam up there, with yaks and porters, and teams of hikers moving up and down the steep, narrow slope that leads up to and then beyond the bridge on the other side. We single-file it up to the bridge, where we wait for a yak team to pass, and I get ready to move across the bridge as fast as I can while Meenakshi stays behind to take some pictures.

I cinch up the tie of my hat to keep it from blowing into the river and try to move across without looking down. I fail, and for a moment I'm in the middle of the bridge, hundreds of feet above Everest's wash, wind-blown and scared and small.

The moment is captured on video by Meena. I stop, look to my right, then down the valley, my foot suspended in air, wavering, my left hand clutching the cable rail. It's only a split second, then I move on, a sleepwalker, a dream, a millisecond of air and mountain and steel and flesh all together as one.

The climb up the triangle to Namche begins immediately and for the next two hours is relentless. Endless switchbacks lead to more switchbacks lead to long straightaways lead to stone steps. It's all up. Around every turn is a view across or down the valley where we came. The roars of the dueling rivers lift up from the valley like songs.

We cross paths over and over with a group of three Australian women and their bemused Nepali guide as they struggle against gravity and the endless slope. I keep pace with the older of the three women, as she moves painfully slowly, but then discover I don't have to worry. The women have already climbed Kilimanjaro.

Up ahead, Meenakshi chats amicably with the ladies' porter. He tells her that just a few years ago she would not have been able to find a room in one of the Western lodges at all. So tailored to Westerners has the Nepali tourism industry been that only recently have "locals" begun to explore their own country.

The trail continues and the weather worsens as we climb into the fog. My altimeter passes 10,000 feet, then 10,500, then 11,000. I move slowly, still feeling not quite right from my flu, and not wanting to burn out on Day Two.

The altitude and the weight on my back make my knees sluggish, and it begins to feel as though an anchor is tied around my waist.

The trail swings us around the base of the southern foot of the horseshoe that is Namche and finally, after two solid hours of hauling, as the temperatures drop and our lungs begin to wonder where the oxygen has gone, we see signs of life: the outskirts of Namche.

We walk by an old Sherpa home, and several children see Meenakshi's hands and circle around her, teasing. One asks her, "Is he your husband?"

A few minutes later, we come upon another army checkpoint and have to show our trekking permit and park pass. Outside the police hut is a map showing Namche as directly above us, though from here we can't see anything except mist.

We choose to go around the edge of the ridge and approach the town from the front. The trail is carved directly into the side of a very steep slope and drops literally all the way down to the river to our left. We come to a turn in the trail, Meena in the lead, and incredibly, a baby cow appears to be waiting for us in the middle of the path. The calf sidles up to Meena, who extends her hand, and the cow gives her a quick lick. Behind them the mist and fog pour down from the mountain tops, and below them, the sound of the river can still be heard faintly.

A week ago on the streets of Kathmandu, a passing baby cow also licked my hand.

This is an incredible stroke of luck, as being licked by a cow is a harbinger of prosperity and fortune, by Nepali tradition. As if the Goddess Lakshmi is leading us to a golden fortune, we round the turn and there it is, Namche Bazaar, the Sherpa capital.

It is stunning. For a very long time, Meenakshi and I stand at the entryway looking up at this amazing place, high on the U-shaped flank of a sacred mountain, a week's walk from the nearest car.

The town is terraced and built on a half-circle valley, like an amphitheater, rising up to a distant ridge. The feet of either end of the half circle drop straight down into the mist. Namche Bazaar is the center of Sherpa culture, a commercial tourist resort and a marketplace where traders from as far away as Tibet come weekly to sell, share and barter. Nearly all goods in the Everest region come from or go through Namche.

The tinkling of stonemasons' hammers is as permanent a sound as yak bells, as the town hurries to keep up with trekker demands for more lodges and restaurants.

Two- and three- and four-story buildings rise up on the circle, with colored tin roofs and painted windowsills. A huge stupa (a kind of memorial) greets visitors near the gateway where we stand. A little farther up the main path into town, a thin stream engineered down the hill is being used for washing clothes and dishes and for drink.

It's jarring to see this activity and feel the energy of this mad town hanging on the side of a massive cliff.

And as we stand and gawk, the weather seems to change under us and the sweat I've accumulated from the climb begins to dry. It gets cold. We have to move.

We have no clue where we'll stay that night, but the options seem endless and it's only four p.m. We head up the hill into town, walking to the left of the stupa and spinning the prayer wheels clockwise as we go.

I'm suddenly tired, and as we climb up into the narrow cobbled streets and the mass of tourists and locals closes in I begin to feel claustrophobic—an ironic turn after all the space of the valley.

Finding a lodge turns out to not be that easy. We walk randomly, but the first couple we try are booked. So we split up and Meenakshi tries one side of the street while I ply the other.

"Over there," a Sherpa woman in a gear store shouts over to me as I approach. She's pointing across the street to the Yak Hotel. "Rooms over there."

As if on cue, Meena steps out from the Yak Hotel and calls to me, "They have space here!" I look up at the yak skull above the doorway, wrapped in a Tibetan ceremonial khata, a scarf that symbolizes goodwill and compassion.

I chuckle to myself. Looks like we've found our home for the next two days.

Chapter 4
~
Namche Days

The summer of 1985 had been unusually warm in the Khumbu.

Melt from the glaciers had swollen the lakes, many of which were topped out. Cold, deep blue waters crested, or nearly crested, the lips of the lakes. One such lake, the Dig Cho, fifty miles west of Namche Bazaar, drains from the Langmoche Glacier and makes its way past Namche by way of the Bhote Koshi. On August 4, 1985, an enormous chunk of rock and ice broke off the glacier and splashed down in Dig Cho Lake.

The result of that environmental catastrophe was my being able to eat the most delicious plate of momos I'd ever tasted by the light of the electric lamps of the Yak Hotel and Restaurant in Namche.

I knew nothing of that fateful summer twenty-five years ago, but I was comfortable, surrounded by friends and porters and enjoying the wonderful attentions of the host and hostess of the Yak.

First, the momos.

There was a time not so many years ago that I had no idea what a momo was. Now, that seems like saying there was a time before computers, or corrupt politicians. I can no longer imagine my life without momos. For those unfortunate enough to be without: A momo is the Nepalese version of the dumpling, the pierogi or the ravioli—you get the idea. It can be filled with chicken, veggies or other morsels, and most Western versions come with a side of spicy and flavorful sauce for dipping.

Being Tibetan, these had no sauce, and they did not need it. The Yak Hotel chicken momos were sweet and moist and steamed to perfection. The chicken was tenderized with spices and the wrapper was steamed to a pleasant golden glow. I washed it all down with milk tea. The cost of ten momos and a tea? Four hundred rupees. The cost of our room for the evening? Three hundred rupees.

I knew that the days ahead would be hard, and neither of us really knew if we'd be able to make it. But we did know that we'd found our happy place at the Yak, a lodge of incredible luxury compared to what we would face in the days ahead. Space heaters instead of yak dung stoves. Western-style toilets that flushed. A sink with a mirror, and running water to wash in. And, most amazing of all, electricity.

In 1985, when that massive chunk of ice from the Langmoche tumbled into the Dig Cho, it created what geologists call a glacial lake outburst flood. A gigantic tidal wave tore open the side of the lake and sent millions of gallons of glacier water into a tributary that led directly into the Bhote Koshi.

The flood raged into the valley, destroyed fourteen bridges and ravaged eighty kilometers of cultivated land.

Five years earlier, the Austrian government had broken ground on a hydroelectric plant just down river from the Dig Cho. The plant was a wonder of human ingenuity, designed to tame the Bhote and withstand a river flow of one hundred meters per second.

The mountains were having none of it.

The Langmoche flood generated a flow volume of an unheard of 2,000 meters per second. The hydro station was annihilated.

Three years later, when Austria and Nepal tried again, they set the plant higher up the river bank and higher up the valley, in Thame. Namche, only a couple miles distant, would be the main benefactor, and this time, engineers had a better understanding of what the Khumbu was capable of.

Namche got lucky again, in part because the new project became a comedy of errors. Materials were to be transported through Calcutta, but a trade-treaty crisis with India inflated the cost of shipping. Monsoons damaged the penstocks. There were turbine design faults and substandard electrical installations. Over and over, heavy icing during the winter resulted in downed lines and outages.

After spending more than $83 million, the Austrians had had enough, and that's where Namche came in. Though the plant is owned, on paper, by the state, the locals control it. And they control it well.

Namche is a kind of Free-Stater region—distrustful of government, self-sufficient and willing to do its own work.

Because it's so cut off from Kathmandu, Namche does actually work.

In order for the plant to make money, village businesses pay a set rate for power as opposed to rates being based on usage. This means that the price stays the same in the winter and during peak tourist season.

And clean, reliable power meant that my momos were prepared in modern facilities and faster than in most other villages. It meant that the power stayed on and the lodge was clean and fresh, even by obscene Western standards. It meant that I could use a private, warm bathroom. It also meant that I would be back.

Electricity made Namche the center of the Khumbu universe.

So that morning, flush from a hearty breakfast of eggs and beans, and feeling better with a good night's sleep, we fasten on our day-packs and head up the slope, toward the Namche ridge. Our plan is to climb up about 1,200 feet and spend several hours at a higher altitude before hiking back down to Namche, the classic strategy for becoming used to altitude.

The day is warm and blue, and across the valley, 20,299-foot Kongde Ri is floating mysteriously in and out of clouds.

At only four miles away, the mountain's west ridge looks massive in Namche, a chunky, flat wall of extended ice. And even though the mountain is classified as a trekking peak, it's considered a difficult climb. So much so that the government charges $350 for a permit, and the first all-Nepalese team didn't reach the summit until 1975.

We hike slowly up Namche's southern border trail, past a tiny library building and a large army barracks that takes up a sizable portion of Namche's western flank. After twenty minutes we come to the suburb of Chhorkung, where there is a Sherpa museum and another huge triangular mani stone marking the head of the trail that climbs straight up the ridge above Namche.

The going is slow, but the views are spectacular. Below us, the amphitheater of Namche is revealed, colored tin roofs spreading out along the ridge like colored dots. At our backs, the valley drops down and zigzags along the broken ridges back toward Lukla.

Ahead of us and all around rise the tips and flanks of ice amid swirl-ing clouds.

The ridge is saturated with prayer flags, seemingly at every cairn and corner of the trail. If there is a rock, it seems it's tied with prayer flags. They are strung from side to side, up and down the trail, over huge swaths of the ridge. At times, as we seek views along the climb, we have to crawl under strings of prayer flags.

In the pocket of my jacket I carry one prayer flag, a royal blue memory flag dedicated to a friend I call my sister who is fighting cancer. It has her name on it, and I plan on carrying it all the way to Kala Patthar.

Tibetan prayer flags do not carry prayers to the gods, how-ever. That's a standard misconception among Westerners. Rather, the flags are used to promote peace, compassion and wisdom. It is believed that the prayers and mantras on the flags will be blown by the wind to spread that peace and compassion to all pervading space. This explains the staggering number of prayer flags in the region.

As the flag fades from exposure to the elements, the prayers become a permanent fixture in the universe and Tibetans renew their hopes for peace by mounting new flags next to the old, a sym-bol of welcoming life's changes.

Once again, I'm amazed at how readily, and in fact eagerly, peo-ple here accept the circle of life. There is no struggle here, only ancient tradition renewed over and over.

Life moves, life moves on. Deal with it.

And so we move on also, slowly, and a group of Japanese tourists holding umbrellas passes us.

We're moving up to 12,500 feet today, but without as much struggle as in yesterday's hill climb. We still move slowly and delib-erately, but our breath comes easier in the misty mountain air.

Suddenly, with a tremendous roar, a Twin Otter breeches the cliff over our heads and goes tearing down the valley. We're near the airport!

The tiny Syangboche Airport at the top of the thick ridge makes Lukla Airport appear modern. Its dirt runway blows up dust and debris. At this height it is one of the highest commercial airports in the world, but except in an emergency (or if the money is right) it does not cater to tourists.

Mostly, it moves supplies. Its biggest client is the Everest View Hotel on the other side of the mountain and our destination for the day.

Meenakshi and I clamber up a large rock near the end of the runway to watch the planes take off into the valley. In the West this would never be allowed, to be this close. Here it's something to do to pass the day.

We don't wait long before a plane, a Tara Air Otter like the one that brought us to the valley, comes barrelling down the runway, its engine at full throttle, and lifts off over the hands of screaming children and sightseers who have packed the end of the runway. We watch the plane turn hard right into a cloud and make a beeline toward the passes.

After a little while of kicking around the airport, it begins to get cold and a fine mist has dropped onto the ridge. We bundle up and begin the climb up to the Everest View Hotel, or so we think.

The hotel seems down on its luck, with paint needed here or there and not much of a view—the clouds make sure of that. We walk around the yard for a while and notice a sign drawing attention to the views, but there are none.

Down the ridge a little ways is a pleasant enough plot of grass, and we sit at the edge of the path, the river roaring down below, and relax, taking in the scenes and wondering if the clouds will move.

After about ten minutes of this, we're told by a passing hiker that the Everest View Hotel is "that way." He points further along the patch.

"What's that, then?" I ask, pointing to the rundown hotel we passed.

He shrugs and moves on. So, once again, so do we.

We follow the narrow path around the inside edge of a steep ridge and up a little rise until we see a low, dark structure in the distance.

The hotel is clean and huge, completely out of place and time for this valley.

The Japanese-owned Everest View Hotel is by far the largest consumer of electricity in the Khumbu, with a 30-kilowatt connection. Guest rooms are warmed by electric space heaters. There's hot water in the bathrooms, and there are hairdryers! There is a TV in the lodge, though a television signal has not yet made it there, so people watch videos. Oxygen is available in all the suites.

The setup is sweet. Trans Himalayan Tours owns the Everest View and is a representative of Overseas Courier Services, kind of a UPS for the world. As such, they pretty much have a monopoly on the goods that come in through the airport, which they call theirs.

The hotel itself reminds me of a low, wide Frank Lloyd Wright prairie house, with long thick bricks and a narrow entranceway that gives way to a large hall. It's still warm enough to eat on the patio, so we order grilled yak cheese sandwiches and tomato soup, as the food at the Everest View is supposed to be some of the best Western available.

We have no views, of course. The clouds have socked in the entire valley and soon will be upon us.

The food is not bad. Not quite what mother makes, but close enough to thoroughly enjoy. We wash it all down with a slice of chocolate cake, and sit back a while until the clouds sink down and an afternoon fog has settled in the valley.

The hike back is simple, though it begins to mist. We meet Jim and his crew halfway to the Everest View and encourage them to continue their hike.

Back in Namche, we enter the town from a different, more secluded point and are able to have a pleasant walk through the locals' gardens and huts. But as we reach a split in the path, two wild horses come roaring by, unchained and unfettered. Later that evening, the horses will create a minor crisis by knocking down a Western tourist. Lodge and shop owners are always upset to see a potential source of income get hurt.

I drop into the cybercafe next to the Yak and make a few posts, then take a short walk around the streets while Meenakshi stops at a bakery for snacks for tomorrow and orders our dinner.

That evening we have rice and dahl for dinner and a side of boiled potatoes. We meet a Polish couple, moving slowly with their guide and porter. We meet a large, loud group of eastern Europeans of whom only half will make it to base camp.

After dinner, we hang out in the common room for a bit, but it's dark now and sleep comes like clockwork. I take a quick walk outside before bed, strolling down the now empty streets. I slip in between two houses to a terraced path somewhat up from the main drag and stop to take a couple pictures of the now sleepy town.

Tomorrow we will leave the comforts of this mad, beautiful town and head to Tengboche and its famous monastery. But we'll be back.

I breathe in the cold, misty air and listen for a few minutes to the light tap of rain against the tin roofs, and the wind ruffling the prayer flags on the ridge above, and I think that this is where I want to be.

Chapter 5

~

The Chill of the Khumbu

The morning is blustery and cold, and it turns out to be the best part of the day.

My pack feels heavier than usual this morning, as we set off up the long, steep stone stairs that take us to the topmost tier of Namche's paths. A fine mist has settled over the village, over the valley, over the Khumbu, and every so often a slight breeze kicks up shards of cold rain and stings our hands and face.

I'm wearing the same clothes I've had on since Lukla (I only carry two sets, and a third change of underwear). They're made of fast-drying material, and I've tucked my shirt and pants deep into my sleeping bag each night, so they're dry. But I'm beginning to notice the smell.

The set of semi-independent Europeans passes us only about twenty minutes into the day. We'll cross paths with some or all of them for most of the journey, but for today, they pass us once and we don't see them again until Tengboche.

Yesterday, we attacked the ridge directly, gaining altitude quickly to force acclimatization. Today, our plan is to move around the long ridge, a thousand feet above the river, at a mellow rate of ascent. The first couple miles are gentle and the trail is an engineering wonder, more graded than anything we've encountered in the White Mountains.

In some areas, where there would normally be a cliff, trail engineers have designed retaining walls to prop up the path, complete with culverts to move water underneath and prevent erosion. It is a thing of beauty, a great wall of Namche, a superhighway 12,000 feet in the air where yak and man and horse and chicken can move, sometimes two or three abreast.

We are able to pay somewhat abnormal attention to the details of the trail because we can see nearly nothing else. The guides describe this section of the trek as being one of the most stunning, with soaring mountain walls in every direction and the majesty of the roaring river below.

We see none of that.

Every once in a while, the mist rolls hard enough to clear a distant peak or we catch a glimpse of a ridge shooting straight up from the fog, but most times it doesn't even last long enough for me to move my camera to my eye.

It is all beautiful and mysterious. Hikers and porters pass with few words. The normal chatty trail talk seems to be subdued in this strange gossamer world, a cathedral of claustrophobia amid unseen wide open spaces.

Far in the distance around several turns and bends in the trail, we see the vague outline of a large stupa. It seems to protrude into the ether, its crown like a beacon in the mist.

It is the Tenzing Norgay chorten, dedicated to the most famous Sherpa in the world. Built in 2003 to commemorate the 50th anniversary of Norgay and Hillary's momentous summit of Everest, it stands on a corner of the path, enormous against the clouds, as large as Norgay's reputation in Nepal.

In the mist and clouds, at this place of near divine worship toward a man of little means who became a symbol to the world of Sherpa moral and physical fiber, we rest.

There are other trekkers here, and a porter stop, and just as we reach the stupa a yak train comes clanging by, but the spot feels as though it maintains a higher karmic value in the universe. It's a place of reflection amid the traffic, a place to consider exactly what all of this is about to begin with.

There's a lot of history lost in the myth of Norgay and Hillary's famous summit. To his very great credit, Hillary spent the remainder of his life giving back to the Khumbu, building schools, educating the Sherpa people, creating greenhouse and farming co-ops. But even a general glance at the actual story of that first summit of Everest makes it clear who the stronger, and perhaps more humble, climber really was.

In fact, Hillary was nearly an afterthought in the famous summit, compared to Norgay.

First though, the Baron. One of the names lost in the shine of the summit accomplishment is that of the guy who got Hillary and Norgay there to begin with, Baron Henry Cecil John Hunt. Hillary was not the leader of the 1953 expedition. Hunt was. A lifelong military man, Hunt was selected to lead the team by SHAEF, the Supreme Headquarters Allied Expeditionary Force. Ah, the British and their titles!

He was already forty-three by the time the team set up base camp, and in typical stiff-upper-lip fashion, he never even considered himself for a shot at the summit. Back then, an expedition was considered a success if even a single member of the team set foot on a summit—a far cry from today's competitive obsession with getting as many clients up there as possible.

Hunt ran the expedition like he was directing an invading army. There were more than 400 people on the "team," and more than 350 of them were porters who carried the 10,000 pounds of baggage from Kathmandu (there was no Lukla airport back then). They arrived in March but didn't even get close to the South Col until late May.

And again, history diverges from myth. Hunt selected his two strongest climbers to make the first push to the summit—Tom Bourdillon and Charles Evans. And they came so close! Evans's oxygen system failed him only 300 vertical feet from the summit of Everest, and the pair turned back.

I've often thought about those two, 300 feet from lifelong fame and fortune, making the decision to turn around and share their information and the path they broke out with the next team. Later, many members of the team said they were unaware that what they were attempting would lead to such glory, that they were simply teammates working on a single goal.

But they knew.

So, enter Hillary and Norgay. New Zealand-born Edmund Hillary was a baby, strong and full of ability but with limited expedition experience. Norgay? It was his seventh attempt at the summit of Everest. One year earlier, as a member of a Swiss expedition, Norgay made it to 28,215 feet, the record at the time. He was already the most famous Sherpa in the world in 1953, and it was Hunt who chose Norgay to pair with Hillary. Not that Hillary minded, as just a few weeks earlier, he had slipped and fallen into a crevasse and it was Norgay who secured the rope and saved Hillary's life.

The two men did not make the attempt alone. They had a support crew of three other men who went up to the South Col with them and set up high camp, keeping them fed and warm and ready for the eventual push to the top. It took two days before all five men climbed up to 27,900 feet and helped Hillary and Norgay set up their final camp.

The next day the two set off wearing 30-pound packs. Remember, there were no fixed ropes then, and when they reached the 40-foot rock face right below the summit, Hillary free-climbed that sucker. It's now known as the Hillary step.

They reached the summit—together, Hillary claimed—at 11:30 a.m. on May 29, 1953. The final historic irony of that day was that the only picture in existence of that momentous occasion is of Norgay on the summit, his ice ax flying the flags of Nepal and Britain. Norgay did not know how to use a camera, and Hillary later said that he felt the summit of Everest was not the place to teach him.

The two men achieved instant world-wide fame, though the British government politely declined to knight Norgay. Later, in his autobiography, Norgay gave Hillary credit for setting foot first on the summit. Hillary denied this and went to his grave insisting the two men summited together.

"It has been a long road," Norgay wrote. "From a mountain coolie, a bearer of loads, to a wearer of coats with rows of medals who is carried about in planes and worries about income tax."

I sit for a few minutes at Norgay's stupa wondering about this man, who in pictures from the '70s wears plaid suit coats and feathered fedoras and is always smiling. The wind and haze lift up off the valley floor, and porters and trekkers amble by. Some are oblivious to the memory they are passing. Others, like myself, stand quietly for a moment in front of the plaque, reading about the "Tigers of the Snow" and stewing in their own thoughts about why they are here.

Someone, in large red letters, has tagged the stupa with the symbol of Lovism, a circular spiral extending up, and a message that reads, "Peace is possible only by true Love."

That seems about right for here and for now. Meena and I snack on yak cheese and gulp down some water, still warm from having been boiled that morning, and as the mist seems to get even thicker and our packs seem to get even heavier, we leave Norgay behind and turn our feet toward Tengboche.

A few trail spurs later, we're on the north side of the Namche plateau. If the skies were to clear, the whole valley would be open before us, with views presumably all the way to Tengboche and beyond to Everest. But we see nothing. In Kenjoma I stop for a quick cup of terrible coffee before we drop through a patch of rhododendrons to a deep cleft in the side of the hill. The trail swings us back around and suddenly we are dropping down into the valley. We pass through Sanasa, where an important trail junction directs some trekkers west toward Gokyo and the Cho La Pass. Next time, I think, next time, I will move in that direction.

For now, we continue a relentless descent, down, down and down we roll, past Lawichasa and Tashinga, tiny mountain hamlets with smoky momo huts and decaying lodges where the children stand in the doorways and the women of the lodges hustle to keep fires burning in the damp air.

We lose 1,000 feet and suddenly there's the Milk River again, roaring like a locomotive. At river's edge is the village of Phunki Thenga, or, as we call it, Funky Tango. Little more than a rest stop, Funky Tango consists of two tiny crowded lodges. We reach one of the lodges just as the weather goes bad for good, and the rain begins to come down with authority.

It is cold, and the place feels tired, and moisture begins to seep into the folds of my clothes. My sweat becomes cold and my legs feel wooden.

We have to make up that lost altitude to reach Tengboche, but right now I just want to sit and give my knees a break. Jim's crew is already in the Cozy Garden Lodge, which at that moment is anything but cozy or garden-like, but we don't care. My pack crashes to the floor and a few people slide over to make room for us at a bench near the door. Trekkers are crammed in here elbow to elbow, each of them looking anxiously out the window as the rain continues and the temperature drops.

No one is staying there that night, but no one wants to hike up that hill either.

We order noodle soup and tea, figuring the wait for such simple food will be short. We're right—a large pot seems to be ready and waiting. The iron stove is roaring in the small kitchen and flames lick out the sides as the lodge owner and either his daughter or wife struggles to keep the food coming.

I warm my cold hands on the side of the bowl and breathe in the deep stocky aroma of onions, cabbage and carrots.

The soup bowl is dirty and chipped, and the onions and carrots crunch as I bite them, but it doesn't matter. I'm chilled and dreading that climb and the soup is warm and the onions are sharp. I don't even bother checking the silverware anymore, and three heaping spoonfuls into my lunch I can feel my energy and morale returning. I find myself devouring the soup, slurping it down in a veggie orgy of tingly goodness. I tip the bowl up to my lips once the noodles are gone and drink the remaining broth as an offering to that wet, muddy hill that sits waiting for us outside the window. I discover Meena has downed her soup even faster than I and we share a wordless laugh as our energy and enthusiasm return in that beat-up truck stop with its dirty dishes and cracked windows at the bottom of a massive ravine.

By this time, most of the other trekkers have left and we're able to take our time gearing up for what's ahead. I strip off my now dirty and wet shirt and replace it with a warmer Techwick one. I tuck my pants into my wool socks in an effort to keep out the water, and decide to begin the climb wearing a light L.L.Bean windbreaker, figuring the effort of the climb will keep my body temperature up and my wide-brimmed rain hat will mitigate the dampness from above.

We're ready.

We descend down to a thick, well-built steel and wood bridge, only a few feet from the river, cross and begin our climb up.

There are no villages here, no rest stops and very little cover. After about twenty minutes of a somewhat tree-covered ascent, the trail attacks the slope in short, steep switchbacks and the rain comes down in sheets. I tip my head into the wind, but it doesn't matter.

Before long the hard pack become slick and a light brown fluid mixture of mud and yak dung creates a river of ooze as we navigate the ever steepening climb.

On an open section, I squeeze under some branches of an overhanging tree and pull out my heavy Gore-Tex. It's something I wanted to wait on, but I'm just too cold and I know what hypothermia feels like. I have no intention of ending this journey because I'm too stubborn to take the time to get warm.

With both of us layered up, we continue on, and after another thirty minutes the slope moderates and we swing around one final switchback and there it is. A house-sized kani gate marks the entrance to Tengboche.

We're tired and wet and cold as we drag ourselves through the gate. At 12,700 feet, it's the highest either of us has ever been, but we feel no joy. Instead, the cold sting of the village's plateau wind hits us and it is just a miserable place.

Sheets of clouds swirl down into Tengboche and we stand there for a moment trying to orient ourselves.

Earlier, our lodge owner in Namche called ahead to a place owned by his sister called the Trekkers Lodge and made arrangements for us to stay there. Now, as the wind and rain continue and it begins to get dark, we just want to find a warm stove and maybe some momos.

Without even paying attention to the giant monastery in the center of town, we turn left and head through a small grove of trees and brush and make our way to the edge of the plateau. The Trekkers Lodge is a ramshackle collection of tin and plywood rooms stuck together like broken Legos. A horse stands in the middle of the path, its head down, wet and angry-looking.

My heart sinks. After the luxury of The Yak in Namche, and the grueling three-hour mud climb, the Trekkers Lodge is not what we had hoped for. The inside is not any better. Smoke pours from the badly ventilated stove in the middle of the room, coating the eating area in a thin layer of haze. The walls are paper thin and the kitchen nearly medieval in design and function. One of the Europeans we met yesterday and who passed us earlier in the day is bent over a broken stone wall near the door, retching, her companion patting her on the back trying to ease her suffering.

Even worse, in our eagerness to just get a room and get warm, we make a terrible mistake—Meenakshi asks for the room in Nepali.

The owner, thinking her to be either a presumptuous porter or, even worse, a local, hands her a key and walks off without a word, and refuses to give her blankets.

Our "room" is a horror. Hanging precipitously on the edge of the plateau cliff like a tin shed, and reached only from the outside, the tiny room barely fits two. To get to it we have to hug the edge of the building, stepping over rain buckets and rocks. The room is musty and dank, the mattresses are wet and the walls are crawling with spiders.

We are prepared for discomfort, but this is just dangerous.

We dump our gear and walk back across the plateau. There are half a dozen lodges in Tengboche, and they are all booked.

We're out of options. But as we left the Trekkers Lodge, I noticed that several of the rooms abutting the dining area were unoccupied. While they're not much warmer, at least their occupants would not have to worry about falling off a cliff while taking a pee break in the middle of the night.

So I act like a Westerner, and without Meenakshi at my side, I explain in a loud voice to the lodge owner that our room is overrun with spiders, we have no blankets even though I saw an unused pile near the stairs and as a paying American I would like an upgrade right this minute, pretty please.

Without a word, he gives me everything I ask, and I suddenly feel both victorious and like a jerk at the same time.

No matter, at least tonight there will be no spiders.

Chapter 6
—
The Busiest Ghost Town

There should not be any people here who aren't monks. But there are, lots of them.

We try to make the best of our situation at the Trekkers Lodge, but it's not easy. Outside, rainy mist blows, then settles, then blows again over the plateau that is Tengboche.

We do discover that the group of Europeans is also in the Trekkers Lodge with us, but the place is a wreck. The common room stove is spitting out a dusty mix of soot and smoke, smearing the windows and giving the whole place a slightly seedy look. It's also cold and the stove itself isn't retaining much heat.

Though we manage to talk the owner into giving us a room near the common space (and deal with the porters joking that there are spiders in Europe as well), the space isn't dry or warm, and it will be noisy.

So, faced with the prospect of being cold and miserable inside the Trekkers Lodge, or being cold and miserable out on the plateau, we choose outside.

There are still a couple hours of daylight left and we're hungry, so the first order of business is to find something to eat inside someplace that's warm.

Tengboche plateau is, perhaps, the size of a football field, with steep drops all around (cliffs in some areas) and allegedly surrounded by some of the most beautiful mountains in the world. We don't see any mountains, but I can feel them, oppressive and bitter and icy. Sometimes the wind blows hard enough so we can see a ridge or white cornice and it looks hard and angry.

In the middle of the plateau is the monastery, its steep steps rising up out of the cold wet grass, decorated on all sides by colorful reliefs and long ornamental drapes.

At 12,664 feet, Tengboche is only about 1,400 feet higher than Namche, but it has become the rest stop of choice on the Everest Base Camp trek. The steep climb up to the plateau coupled with the presence of the monastery has created an artificial village, full of merchants and lodges and museums, and of trekkers using those accommodations. But aside from the monks, who number anywhere between thirty and one hundred depending on the season, no one actually lives in Tengboche. So it looks a little like one of those fake colonial villages, all facade. Without the monastery, there would be no village. But because of the monastery, the village is cold and distant, an eroding shell of what a real village might look like, of what the wonderful village we just left does look like.

It is not the Tengboche that Baron John Hunt saw in 1953 on his famous expedition when he wrote that Tengboche "provides a grandstand beyond comparison for the finest mountain scenery that I have ever seen, whether in the Himalaya or elsewhere."

Actually, it's all unpleasant.

Meenakshi and I skip the monastery for now, though we can hear the siren-like chants of the monks inside the main temple and smell sweet incense. We move counterclockwise around the plateau instead, saving the monastery for last. There are half a dozen lodges, a few trinket stores, a bakery and an Internet cafe. The monastery sits slightly up on a hill, enclosed by the monks' own lodges and a large, beautifully carved archway.

The tourist lodges are crowded and dank. The trinket stores are junk. The Internet cafe is closed. We stop at the bakery, a tiny island of warmth and sanitation amid the madness, and take a few minutes to warm up, guzzle a whole container of lemon tea and share an apple strudel that is undercooked but still sweet and refreshing enough to lift our spirits somewhat.

After, we head off in different directions to see if we can find some information about Pheriche, tomorrow's destination, and our first real test of height and endurance.

We've been lucky so far finding lodges as we go, but now as the villages become smaller and the tour groups begin crowding out solo trekkers we need to be more savvy about our lodging.

Outside the bakery, I meet Lene Oh, waiting for his lone client to catch up.

"Oh, hey, hey over there," he calls out to me, singling me out from fifty feet away. "Oh! How can I help you?"

I assume at first he's one of the lodge owners. He's a slight man. His deeply creased face shows years of sun and ice. But he grins and his teeth zigzag like stalactites and he extends his hand. It's an unusual gesture for a Nepali and it puts me at ease.

"Is this your lodge?" I ask.

"Ohhhhhhh no, no, no, no!" He laughs as though I've just made the most wonderful joke. Perhaps I have and don't know it. "I'm waiting for my client. But I can help you. Come in, come on. Oh! I'll buy you coffee."

Not tea? This guy's good. I follow him into a tiny lodge at the edge of the plateau. It's just as horrible as our lodge, a dirty gaggle of porters and single trekkers sitting along long rows of plywood tables that are propped up by wooden sawhorses. Everybody stares at me when I walk in—like in a spaghetti Western.

"Sit, sit," Lene says, then fishes out a torn slip of paper from his pocket and writes down his name, then amazingly, his email address. I just stare at it. "Kathmandu!" he says, by way of explanation. "I have an apartment there. Nothing much. A computer though!"

He pauses, then adds, "Oh! When there's power!"

His English is very good and I tell him that, and he beams and nods. Then, under his email address he writes "Nagarkot Guest House."

"What's that?" I ask.

"Where you will stay in Pheriche!"

So he's a mind reader too. He has sized me up as unattached to a commercial tour group, figures I'm not dirty or miserable enough to be heading back yet, and knows I'm going to need a place to stay. All true. All excellent deductions.

His client finally catches up to us, a single Japanese man, stout, breathing heavily, with a wide-brimmed tan hat that looks like something Gilligan would wear. Lene Oh introduces us, but I forget his client's name and he does not know English and I do not know Japanese so we just nod.

The exhausted Japanese man turns abruptly and throws himself down in the corner of the lodge, done apparently with both of us for the day.

Lene Oh turns his attention back to me. "We go up there tomorrow. I'll tell them you're coming, yes?"

I have no idea how much it's going to cost me, but Pheriche is a long ways off, and I'm tired and if this little 50-year-old man with a road-map face can have a room ready for us when we get there, I'm game to try.

"Yes!" I say. "For two. Me and my wife."

"Oh!" Lene Oh says and actually looks over my shoulder, as though Meenakshi might have been standing there all along. "Oh!"

I decline the coffee and Lene Oh walks out with me, happily buzzing with stories of his travels and his family, which is someplace in Pokhara. He's here for the trekking season, moving back and forth with a client here or a client there. He never asks me if I need a porter, something I feel slightly proud of, as though he knows I don't.

We meet Meenakshi outside, and I introduce them. Lene Oh casts down his eyes and becomes suddenly withdrawn, a reaction Meena gets from quite a few Nepali porters and locals on the trail, all men of course.

"OK, Lene," I say. "How much, what do you need to save us a room?"

"Oh! Oh!" He laughs again. "Oh, no! I know the people, they happy to have you. No worries, OK?"

"OK."

And he's off, practically skipping back into the lodge. I turn to Meenakshi and shrug. Either I've secured a room the next town over, or Lene is the leader of a band of trail bandits who now knows our exact schedule and location. Either way, it ought to make tomorrow more interesting.

It's getting on toward evening and the mist that has settled over the plateau is a swirling gray and dark green. We make a quick stop inside the monastery gift shop and museum. Think about that for a moment. More than a week's walk from the nearest road at nearly 13,000 feet, in the middle of the Khumbu Valley, in a village with no residents, is a gift shop.

It is called the Sacred Land Visitors Eco-Center and it is surreal. There is a museum about Sherpa culture and a film on Himalayan healing techniques and one on the monastery. The films cost extra.

Primarily, the center sells things—incense, patches, T-shirts, postcards, that type of thing. They have a website. Yes, really. It's www.sacredland.net. The pictures on the site are stunning and, for the record, look nothing like the miserable place we see.

We chat a while with the shopkeeper and are disappointed to hear that the head lama who usually blesses trekkers on their way to Everest Base Camp is not here today. We hope it's not a bad omen.

But the monks are in the middle of their daily prayers and that is something we can observe.

The monastery is a large white and burnt-red structure, sur-rounded by smaller buildings for the monks. Tengboche's history is not as ancient as the mythology swirling behind the monastery would lead one to believe.

Every trekker to the region has come here, as a wayfarer or to be blessed. Every one of them. Because of that, Tengboche has become the central spiritual hub of the Khumbu. Families from all over the region often send their sons here, and once a year a very famous festival draws hundreds to the monastery walls.

But the building we now stand in front of is only seventeen years old.

The first monastery was built on the site in 1916 but destroyed by an earthquake. The second was destroyed by a fire in 1989 that also destroyed most of the monastery's texts and artifacts. With help from a variety of sources, including trekking companies, foreign aid organizations, and yes, Hillary, the stone masonry monastery was painstakingly rebuilt and reopened in 1993.

A massive archway, filled with ornate carvings, greets visitors as they climb the steps to the courtyard, the site of festivals and many outdoor ceremonies.

As we walk up to the main doorway, leading to the dokhang, or prayer hall, we can hear the hum of monks chanting prayers.

At the foot of the doorway, we're greeted with a stone with the foot-shaped imprint of Sange Dorje, the flying lama. Sange is credited with bringing Buddhism to the Khumbu with his supernatural flights through the valley!

Much to our chagrin, we have to remove our boots before entering the prayer hall. But we need not worry about our own odors, as the area around the chanting monks is packed with trekkers, and the smell, a mix of sweat, incense and feet, is very nearly overwhelming. It is so strong, it seems as though you can feel the air around you.

Despite the awful smell, the prayer hall is exquisite. We slide quietly into a far corner to watch the proceedings. A two-story-high golden statue of Shakyamuni Buddha, or the Buddha of the Present, takes up most of the front of the hall. Rows of monks in brightly colored red and orange robes sit along the other three sides. Some of them read from long scroll prayer books. Some have the prayers memorized and chant with their eyes closed, swaying slightly. A few young monks, not used to the attention of tourists, roll their eyes and snicker to each other. The prayer hall is absolutely packed with trekkers, but the monks are deep in prayer, and their words are like a low, steady hum, the human equivalent of the sound of a Tibetan prayer bowl. Their chants are hypnotic, and aside from a few camera clicks and the ever present trekker cough, the hall is mostly quiet.

I try to focus on the chant, to sit a little straighter and meditate along with the drone of the words. But I can't. I'm unable to remove myself from the smell. But mostly, I'm horrified by the number of trekkers in that room, all of them most likely heading to the same place we are heading tomorrow.

After about ten minutes, I share a knowing glance with Meenakshi and we get out of there—from the oppressive heat and smell of the prayer room back out to the frigid mist of the Plateau.

It's dark now and we snap on our headlamps and slowly pick our way back to the Trekkers Lodge.

And while the lodge is terrible and our dinner stale and unfilling, and we can't get warm and smell like yak dung, we do spend the evening chatting with Tim and Karen, the two solo trekkers we met on our first day. It's nice to be able to end our day with these two amicable and upbeat souls, both of them attempting the same trek in the same manner with the same fears and crazy enthusiasm as us.

There is a pleasant older French couple there as well. They are on their way down, so hold a fair amount of interest and credibility to the others in the room. I ask them some questions about weather and lodging, but alas they know very little English. It's the first time in my life I wish I knew French.

Elsewhere the group of half a dozen young Europeans appears to be having a grand time. One woman from Ireland speaks too loudly and can't stop talking about her other trips and how surprised she was by how dirty things are here. Another is wrapped in a down parka and goes on and on about how he has to share a room with the one from Ireland, and hopes the locals aren't scandalized by this apparent digression of decorum. I overhear another woman off-handedly remark that she has brought fourteen pairs of underwear with her, one for each day. Her porter, presumably the one carrying the two weeks of underwear, just smiles.

I wonder where the ill woman is. In bed I hope.

It all wears me down, and I wish we could sleep but our room is so close to the common area that the noise would prevent that. So we just tuck in with our tea and chat and swap stories with Tim and Karen until the Europeans have nothing more to talk about and begin to float off to bed. The porters either slink off to their tents or head out to the spider room we abandoned, and that's our signal to do the same.

It's been a long day, but we resolve to skip breakfast tomorrow morning in order to get a jump on these people and make a run for Pheriche ahead of the rest.

Before I turn in, I snap on my headlamp and walk around to the back of the building to use the outhouse. It's nearly snowing now, and as I stand on the edge of the cliff, looking back on the Namche Valley, the silver and white rain flakes mix with the twinkle of stove lights thousands of feet down in the valley and the whole Khumbu seems to melt into a smear of mist and uncertainty.

Tomorrow we'll be five days into our journey, and we've yet to see Everest or any sign of the upper Khumbu mountains. I whisper a silent prayer up there on that plateau, asking the mountains to reveal themselves, but feel foolish doing so.

I apologize to the air for being anxious, and resolve to be more patient. The mountains are here. We have time.

Chapter 7

~

Freezing in Pheriche

I wake to the sound of snoring Sherpas. To be fair, the tired Nepalis sprawled out along the common-area benches are likely porters from outside the Khumbu.

It's 5:30 a.m. and we pack quietly in the cold and slink out of the lodge before our host knows we're gone. There's no contract—written or otherwise—that ties us to eating breakfast at the Trekkers Lodge, but we don't wish to be asked because we don't want to say no.

Tengboche is asleep, and clouds and mist hang low over the valley, making it darker than it actually is.

The fog of my breath swirls before my eyes as we move over the wet, frosty Tengboche plateau. I'm very cold despite my Gore-Tex shell. We walk quickly, hoping the weight on our backs will generate some warmth.

The trail drops down off the plateau and once again we find ourselves facing a long, steep descent to the river. We had left the Milk River yesterday as we had rounded the bend behind Namche, and now the plan was to follow the Imja Khola to the Pheriche Valley.

The word "Khola" denotes a tributary of the main branch, while "Imja" is a word we heard used to describe Island Peak—in other words, a branch of the island—but the terms are far from certain.

As dismal as Tengboche is now, the plateau must be glorious in the springtime. The trail takes us through an enormous rhododendron forest—the bushes tower over our heads. In some sections we walk under the overhanging branches of the shrubs and drooping moss.

It's like some fairy land, every inch packed with the flowering tree.

With more than thirty flowering species in Nepal, it's no wonder the rhododendron is the country's official flower. Rhododendron Arboreum is the most renowned species, prized for its bright red flowers.

Red is an auspicious color in Nepal, used for blessing tikas (the customary marks of powder worn on the forehead) and for the saris worn by brides during weddings. Red will play a role in our day as well.

Today is the high day of Deshain, the enormous and important Nepali festival that can last anywhere from four to fifteen days depending on who you ask and what region you're in.

Earlier in the year, Meenakshi and I had to wait for the date of our Kathmandu wedding to be decided by when the first day of the festival was to take place. It was a frustrating couple weeks, as the timing of our trek, not to mention airfare, waited on a variety of consultations, primarily involving lunar calculations. Finally, it was decided that Deshain 2010 would begin on October 8, so that was the day of our wedding. That makes today Dashami, or the day of blessings, when young ones visit elders and receive tika blessings.

In her backpack Meenakshi carries a small pouch of red tika, and my plan is to celebrate this high holiday by presenting her with a tika blessing somewhere along the trail today. We just have to find the right place.

In the meantime, we pass through a series of villages about 500 feet above the river. In Deboche, villagers are setting up trinket booths along the trailside. In Changme Teng a large trekking group is just waking, ruffled bed heads popping out of tents and sleepy white men in long johns and boots stumbling to the tall blue tent that serves as a latrine. And in Milinggo, we are startled by a porter, running fast, desperate for something.

He has lost his yaks, he explains, five of them, including a white one. Have we seen them? I'm too startled by the thought of someone losing their yaks to answer. Meenakshi says that no yaks have passed us, white or otherwise. He runs on, and we both burst out laughing.

The morning passes pleasantly. We enjoy two solid hours on the trail alone before we begin to see signs of trail life, locals out for a morning stroll, then porters with trekker gear on their backs, then the yak trains, then the trekking groups.

By the time we reach the thick, steel trestle bridge that carries us to the west side of the river, we've lost nearly 1,000 feet, and from the center of the bridge we can look up the valley and see the trail begin to climb again, steeply, up to Pangboche. We will regain the lost feet and gain another hundred before lunch.

There's nothing to do but climb.

We don't talk much, Meenakshi and I, each lost in thought. Occasionally, between my own heavy breaths, I hear the sound of her cough, or a boot splash in a mud hole. The trail becomes a meditation in itself. Waterfalls cascade thousands of feet all around us. The river rushes, white noise behind our footsteps. A white shaggy yak, its head low, mud and water dripping over its eyes and fur, comes ringing by. I put my head down to the mist and watch its filthy hooves as it passes by, wondering if this is somehow the lost white yak.

The trail twists up the valley wall in tight switchbacks, and mani stones and mani walls rise up on either side of us. Huge weather-blistered stupas break out of the mist. Their Buddha eyes watch us come and watch us go.

It's hypnotic, a morning of rain and valleys and mist, of prayer flags and mountain walls all around. We climb. We climb. We climb.

Finally, after one more long series of steps, we come to a kani archway jammed into a mountain pass. The slope levels out and we are at the height of land for now. We stop to catch our breath and take pictures. I'm exhausted, but we've made good time and I'm pleased to see Pangboche come into view just ten minutes later.

The path takes us up the side of the town. Lower Pangboche is all terraced yak pastures. Upper Pangboche is lodge after lodge. By now, the village is awake and children play in the dirt, watching us pass. At what appears to be the top of the final rise, we pick a long, colorful lodge right on the trail and duck inside for our late breakfast.

We're waited on by a young man in red and orange robes. He's studying to become a monk at Tengboche Monastery but is working at his family's lodge for the holiday. He's polite, and quiet and smiles at us, and we sink into an order of Tibetan flatbread with fried eggs like it's the only food on the planet.

As we eat, we are overtaken by the main wave of trekkers coming from Tengboche. It's like a parade, but instead of getting discouraged by the fact that it took them all only four hours to catch up to us, we watch the familiar faces and bet on who will make it and who won't.

The Europeans pass us by, walking hard, talking loudly. The woman who was ill is on her feet and walking strongly. She'll make it. The one in the parka, though, no way. Tim and Karen pass us by and we crank open a window and wave. They will certainly make it. There is the group of hardbody Germans we saw in the airport, and we're surprised to see them being portered. There's the middle-aged woman, trekking solo and slowly, whom we saw the first day. There's a team of singing Greeks, a dozen men, each with a magnificent mustache. There is a large Polish team, all dressed in red, planning an excursion to Island Peak.

We even see Lene Oh and his Japanese client pass by.

We marvel at the number of faces we recognize. It's like we're all part of the same team now.

After our meal, near an old broken-down water wheel at the outskirts of town, we stop for a water break and meet Mankumar Tamang. Or rather, he meets Meenakshi.

Not yet twenty and working as a porter for a local guide, Mankumar sees our packs and his eyes light up like dollar-sign-shaped Diwali lights.

He's already under contract with a guide, but both his guide and their mutual client are a day behind him.

Mankumar is sick with the flu, already carrying at least his body weight, and is wearing sneakers. But nothing stops him. He tells Meenakshi that he can certainly carry at least one of our packs to Pheriche.

It's rare to find a porter who is actually from the Khumbu, and Mankumar is native to the Lukla area. He fully understands the economy of the Sherpa and he is doing everything he can to take advantage of it.

"It's not going to be easy for you further up," he tells Meenakshi. "It is going to get very hard."

I don't know any of this, of course, because he does not speak English. So off we go, Meenakshi and Mankumar gabbing away about his being a tour leader, and how he makes money, and all the while I begin to feel resentful and restless and start to wish Mankumar would just leave us alone.

The feelings are not logical, as the boy means us no harm and I'm actually interested in his job and his life. But as we climb up a steep rise toward the upper plateau and I feel my breath get shorter and the air get colder, things that Mankumar appears immune to the effects of, I begin feeling like . . . well, a Westerner, like suddenly I don't belong.

"Is he just going to follow us all day?" I snap at Meenakshi.

To both their credit, they see me unraveling and Mankumar jogs on ahead, leaving me to my sour mood.

"Sorry," I mumble.

But at a bend in the trail the boy is waiting for us, and he falls in behind us again. This goes on for about an hour. The information is interesting, but the eager Sherpa begins to get on both our nerves, and Meenakshi finally makes a bargain with him.

If we take his picture and write his information down, in case we ever need his services, he'll continue on without us. We agree, and I wait at the top of a rise in the trail while Meenakshi takes pictures and concludes the arrangement.

"Glad that's over," I say as she catches up to me.

"He's OK," she says. "He's just trying to make some money."

I nod, and we continue, and my mood brightens considerably when in the middle of a long plateau, high above the river, the sun comes out.

We're nearly alone on the trail now, nearing our destination, tired and hungry and aching for views of the mountains, which still won't show themselves, but at least there is sun.

"This is good," Meenakshi says. "This is a good spot."

We walk a little ways off trail and find a flat wide rock. We strip off our packs and toss on our fleece and Meenakshi pulls out her tiny packet of red tika.

There is no easy, or short, way to describe Deshain. Let's just say that the festival commemorates a great victory of the gods over wicked demons and leave it at that.

There are blessings and pot fillings and seed growings and all manner of ritual observations. There is slaughter, oh man is there slaughter—goats, buffaloes, chickens and pretty much anything with four legs and fur (except cows) that Nepalis can get their hands on. And since there is so much slaughter, there is a whole lot of meat-eating as well. There are parades, guns are fired, and ancient temples are open to the public.

But today was the tenth day, the day of the festival that feels the most like Thanksgiving to me, a day when family gathers at the elders' homes to receive their blessing. A day when family comes together to be with each other, to be, well, thankful.

So, on this day, at 13,000 feet, surrounded by mountains I cannot see, on a plateau deeply carved with paths from generations of wanderers from all over the planet, on a flat, warm rock, with yaks grazing in a field behind us, I place tika on the forehead of my wife, and I am as thankful as I have ever been in my life.

About a half hour later, by the time we reach the river split, the sun is gone and our world is cold and barren again. Near the herder village of Tsuro Og, the remainder of our day becomes painfully clear. The Imja jags right and disappears east through a valley toward Dingboche and beyond that to the river's namesake, Island Peak, and its four surrounding glaciers. We know that most of the trekking groups have gone that way as well, as most guide books recommend Dingboche over Pheriche as the day's destination.

That's why we're going in the other direction. Pheriche is smaller, but bound to be less crowded. If Lene Oh has failed to save us a room, our logic is that we'll have less trouble finding an alternate place to stay in the cold, windy Pheriche Valley.

But first we must climb again. Our path splits west, rises up above Tsuro Og and the Loboche River, then makes a sharp right turn up and over a barren rise. Presumably, Pheriche is on the other side of that rise.

Up ahead, high on the hill, I can see the blurry shape of a porter, or perhaps a local woman, with an enormous load on her back. She moves steadily, head down against the wind.

We follow, and it's our first real mistake of the trip. In the wind and mist, and as the day closes in and my thoughts shift to warm lodges and hot tea, I fail to notice an alternate, flat path that swings around the hill instead of over. That is our trail, but we don't know this at the time.

So up we go, again. It's been a long day, and our world is now just freezing mist. As we slowly make our way up that hill, the wind picks up and blows a chill through the Gore-Tex.

It's only a couple hundred feet to the crest, but it takes a long time. It's the first time in our trek that I begin emergency calculations, a mind game I've occasionally had to play in the White Mountains.

What if we can't make it before dark? What if there are no rooms? What if the weather gets worse and we have to find shelter? What if we're lost?

I calculate and hike, and strategize and hike, until we reach a thin plateau topped with an enormous seven-foot-tall chorten, its prayer flags ripped and shredded and hanging off the stones like melting frosting. In that rise, amid the swirling cold mist, we rest and it's a beautiful, frightening place. Higher up, to our left, a ridge appears to continue, along which is a string of smaller chortens. We can see nothing to our right, or ahead, where Pheriche is supposed to be.

I'm heartened to discover a porter rest bench and we take shelter from the wind there to have a snack and try to regain our bearings. Pheriche should be right there, but it isn't, and the trail ahead dips drastically down again into . . . what?

But just as I'm contemplating backtracking down the hill, a group of porters crests the rise and heads right for us. Meenakshi and I hustle our gear off the bench just as they spread out to take a rest, a dirty but happy group of men, smoking and laughing and paying us no mind whatsoever.

Meenakshi asks one where Pheriche is, and he just points ahead and laughs.

So that's where we go. We can only see about ten or fifteen feet ahead of us in the mist, but the Loboche roars below us to the right and I know that the river is our path to the Khumbu Glacier.

We climb down a bit and hear voices to our right. The mist parts long enough to reveal another bridge, also to our right. Our path continues forward, then cuts sharply back to the bridge. Since we know Pheriche is on the north side of the river, we decide to take the bridge. At least we'll be on the proper side!

Once over the bridge, the trail rises up again and crests a short mound. And there it is. A spray of wind hits my face, but I've never been so glad to see the stone walls and broken yak paths of a Khumbu village. Pheriche.

The village is squat and seems to hug a small flat section of earth next to the river, which rages loudly. There is one main path, with perhaps a dozen stone and mud buildings on either side.

As we walk past the first lodge, still on the outskirts of the village, I hear a familiar voice.

"Oh! You made it! Remember me?"

"Lene!" I yell.

We had nearly walked past the Nagarkot Guest House without realizing it. Lene Oh is sitting out in the courtyard, drinking something that does not seem to be tea, out of a mug.

"Yeah yeah!" he says. "Right here! Here's your place."

He came through for us. This crazy little grinning man actually did it. I'm so relieved I want to hug him, but he'd be horrified if I did.

He leads us into the guest house, which is long and flat with a blue corrugated tin roof—a Frank Lloyd Wright prairie-style lodge. It's fairly late in the day and the stove in the common room is already lit. The place smells like cabbage, and it's warm, and porters' clothes hiss with steam by the fire, and a tiny girl with bright red cheeks and a yellow sweater sits in the corner playing with a doll, and it is wonderful.

Lene says a few words to the lodge keeper, a young woman with a bright blue down jacket rolled up to her elbows. She just nods and hands me a key.

"Thank you, Lene," I say, honestly grateful for the time and effort he has saved us.

"Oh sure!" he says cheerfully. "I know them! Kind of far from main town, but quiet right, quiet!"

Our room is clean and dry, a virtual royal palace compared to the Trekkers Lodge, so we dump our gear, pull out our own down jackets and pants, and order our dinner in advance. While it's still light, we walk the hundred yards or so into the main part of town, but it's freezing. A freight train of wind and mist blows right down the center of the main street. Dampness seeps into my jacket and hood.

Another reason for my interest in Pheriche is that it's the location of the Himalayan Rescue Association, an international non-profit hospital and rescue center set up in the '70s to try to reduce the number of casualties in the Everest area. But it's too cold to really explore today.

I make a quick stop at the Internet Cafe, a ramshackle building near the association. But it takes a long time to find the manager and it's expensive, 600 rupees for ten minutes. I post a quick status update and we get out of there.

We have more than an hour to kill before dinner, but it's too cold to do anything except retreat to the lodge and be patient.

For once, circumstance forces us to live by the rules of the Khumbu—patience, conversation, camaraderie. We spend the evening surrounded by a small group of solo trekkers, and it turns into one of the best of the trip.

There is Paul, a hunter and outdoorsman from Wyoming who set about trying to bring his family together by planning a trek for them all to Base Camp. They bagged out, so Paul decided, "The hell with it, I'm going anyway."

There's Karlie, from Ireland, who will be celebrating her 24th birthday in a couple days and who hired her own porter and decided she'd do not just Base Camp but the hard trek over the Cho La Pass, on her own.

There is Lene Oh, and his Japanese client, who sits quietly by the fire and goes to bed hours before any of us or his porters. Later, Lene Oh will casually tell us that he liked talking to us because we talked back.

"He's a good guy, works hard," Lene Oh says of his client. "But he don't say much."

And we are all entertained and charmed by Chori Tenzing. "Chori" means daughter and the little one prefers that title. The lodge keeper's three-year-old is small and stout and puffs out her red cheeks when she wants attention. She takes a particular shine to Meenakshi and the two of them spend the evening chatting about henna and Meena's marriage. The girl is fascinated that Meenakshi knows Nepali, and at one point tells Meenakshi that she did not approve of my growing beard.

I overhear one of the trekkers wonder out loud how anyone could raise a little girl in such an "uncivilized place," the implication being that Tenzing could not possibly be happy.

But she is, as were all the children we passed on the trail. There was no begging and no despair. Many days later we will run across a British trekker who put it best: "These children have nothing, nothing material I mean. But look at them. They may have two marbles between them but they love those marbles—always smiling, always happy. Makes you wonder."

Indeed. I feel a flush of anger at the woman's remark. Am I feeling protective of these people I now am married and inexorably tied to? Do I feel shame at a thoughtless Western attitude? Fatigue and the effects of altitude?

Perhaps it's best explained by paraphrasing Kevin Flynn—maybe she was just messing with my Zen thing, man!

The danger of any long trip to Nepal for a Westerner is not pollution or food poisoning or even Maoists. The danger is romanticism. As I sit by the fire with the porters who have now begun to drink Chang, a cheap form of Nepali moonshine, to celebrate the holiday, and I see Meenakshi buried in her shiny down, playing hand games with a giggling Sherpa child, and the lodge keeper heaps another filthy bucket of yak dung into the roaring stove, and icy wind rattles the flimsy windows and I sip tea so sweet my teeth ache, I find myself feeling so happy and complete and content that I scare myself.

What's going on here? This is not perfection, there is no enlightenment here amid the harsh reality of this place, this lonely outpost near the top of the world where locals scrape by on the backs of ignorant trekkers who judge a child's happiness based on Western standards.

And yet, despite the fact that any one of these people would jump at the chance of a Western education and a McMansion in the 'burbs, they are not unhappy. There is no misery that night. Not from the stinking, hard-drinking porters. Not from our hosts, who are gracious and funny and hard-working. Not from Chori Tenzing, who cheerfully draws pictures of yaks on the windows of the lodge, frosted with condensation.

We gather together that night in the hope of a glimpse of something bigger than ourselves. Mt. Everest, sure. But more than that, something deeper and more transcendental.

And we are close, up here where there are no more trees and the ice is impossibly blue and you can feel your lungs and your heart with every breath, like separate animals inside your chest. Romantic? Sure. But it's been a long trip and our biggest challenges still await. So this night, it *is* romantic, and that's enough.

Chapter 8

~

The Mountains Reveal Themselves

Meenakshi is shouting.

It's six a.m. and I'm a little behind getting up this morning. After a pleasant evening of good conversation in front of a roaring fire, I slept hard, and I need to wrestle first with the toilet before showing my face in the common room.

But as I come down the hall, there is a general commotion of people heading out the door into the cold. Meena is one of them.

"Come on, come out!" she says when she sees me. She takes my hand and leads me out to the courtyard of the lodge. It is absolutely freezing out, and I'm dressed only in Techwick long johns and boots. I have my Gore-Tex shell and hat but no gloves. Her hands are cold.

I step out into the morning glare, and the chill in the air is palpable. It's like walking into a cloud of invisible ice. It takes my stunned body a moment to compensate and I begin shivering almost immediately.

Several trekkers in various states of undress are standing around, all their heads raised to the sky. I step a couple more feet out, away from the lodge, and look up.

We are surrounded by mountains. It literally takes away my breath and I feel dizzy.

In every direction, the silver and white peaks shoot up, ragged spires of misty rock and glaring ice. The sun has not yet risen over the range to the west, but the tips of the peaks all glow a blinding white.

Ama Dablam. Awi. Pokalde. Thamserku. Kangtanga. Some of the names I've memorized and anticipated for days. Others are new, like strange, frightening neighbors. They are all over 6,000 meters.

Directly in front of the lodge the dome of Taboche appears like an enormous white egg cracking right above a still-dark ridge. I don't know what to do or say. I hear the clicking of cameras and the whispered murmurs of other trekkers. Meena has gone back for a camera and I walk up a rise a little bit to get away from the lodge after I realize that my smallest camera, the Olympus, is in the pocket of my jacket.

I film a quick 360, babbling nearly incoherently as it turns out. This is it. We are surrounded by some of the tallest, most beautiful and dangerous mountains in the world. This will be the day of views, the day of walking under the royal blue sky, amid a magical background of mountains.

"Breakfast is ready," Meenakshi says. I'm suddenly hungry and my hands are shaking from the cold, my fingertips ridged and white. Yikes. I jam my hands into my pockets and scurry into the lodge, eager to eat and set out up the ridge for an acclimatization day of rest and picture-taking!

Of course that doesn't happen. One hour later, with full bellies and day packs on, we set out up the ridge toward Dingboche, under a layer of mist and clouds. The mountains have tricked us again, put us in our place, illustrated our tiny stature then gone away, leaving us with a sober understanding of our place in the universe.

But that's fine, as the day is still warm, there's no rain and the fine mist and fog give us occasional views as we climb. On our second and final acclimatization day, we are heading to Dingboche, a larger village just on the other side of the valley bluff.

To reach it, we have to climb straight up a hillock to the north of Pheriche, then down into a series of drumlins on the other side before reaching Dingboche. The town is only about a mile away, but we have to climb about 700 feet, then descend 300 feet, then climb back up to Dingboche at 14,468 feet.

There is no official trail to get over that hump, only some vague beaten paths created by grazing yaks. We take our time, switchbacking up and back and occasionally taking a few tentative steps straight up the rise if our lungs allow it.

It's a pleasant morning. We don't have to worry about trekkers or yak trains. Our day packs feel so light that we spend some time taking videos of red rescue helicopters roaring down the valley. One lands in Pheriche and we watch it come down in a clearing only a few hundred yards from our lodge. We will discover later that the helicopter was there for a porter who broke his ankle coming down the Cho La Pass and was being taken to the Rescue Association for treatment.

After an hour we reach the ridge, out of breath but with no sign of the achy headache or nausea that often accompanies altitude sickness. From this point on, we will have to monitor our conditions carefully for any signs of concern.

I pull out my memory flag for my sister and pause to take a picture. On this ridge that overlooks two villages, surrounded by some of the highest mountains on the planet, we are over 14,500 feet. We are higher than Mt. Whitney, the highest point in contiguous America.

We drop down into a mini-valley, then climb back up and find the official trail leading into Dingboche. It's crowded this morning. The town is the staging village for treks to Island Peak and there's porter and Sherpa activity all around us as we pass by some yak pastures, a huge lodge with "BAKERY" painted on its blue tin roof, and a variety of hole-in-the-wall momo shops.

At the far end of the town I spot a radio tower and figure that's as likely a place as any to have an Internet café. I'm right—Dingboche actually has two of them, right next to each other. One is closed and no one seems to know where its proprietor is. In the other, the young Sherpa owner powers up the generator, which roars like a leaf blower in the suburbs. The connection is terrible, but I manage to leave a status message that suggests this may be the last time I'm able to find a connection before our Base Camp attempt.

For lunch we find a clean lodge high on a rise above town. There we sit at a long row of windows, which warm every time the sun peeks out. The lodge's owner, an old, heavy-set Sherpa woman, sleeps contentedly on an adjoining bench, and a teenager ably takes our order. I'm in the mood for momos and milk tea, while Meenakshi gets a grilled cheese sandwich. We have the place to ourselves in the sun, and my stomach feels strong and I'm happy.

I peel off some of my heavy stinky gear and rest my head on my hand and turn my face to the sun and it's a good day. The lunch is good and we're feeling lazy, and it's tough to hit the trail again, but we want to explore Pheriche a bit before dark, so we head back down.

An enormous team of Canadian teens and twenty-somethings passes us, heading in the other direction, toward an Island Peak summit. They are all dressed in black with matching logos. I gawk. At that age, I had no conception of climbing a 20,000-foot peak, to say nothing of Nepal or even Asia.

We short-cut up a different ridge, wanting to hike a little more west of our lodge in order to enter Pheriche from above. We cut through the back area of a lodge, where we come across a curious sight: several villagers are working an alu pit. A large hole in the still-soft ground has been excavated, and women are carrying bushels full of golf-ball-sized potatoes to the pit, which already is full of thousands of the things. Nepali refrigeration. The frozen earth will be as good a freezer as any for feeding hungry trekkers next season.

We find a beaten trail and follow it up to a large stupa that looks down over Dingboche and are happily surprised to run into Tim and Karen, who are in the middle of their own rest day. They stayed in Dingboche and have hiked much higher than us today, up to an old monastery above the village.

Their plan, like ours, is to head to Loboche tomorrow, but where we will trek through the Pheriche Valley along the river before turning north toward the Khumbu Glacier, they will strike out above the valley and come in nearly level with the glacier.

It's windy up on the rise, so we part with promises to look for each other tomorrow. I know we won't see them, though, as they have proven much faster than us and I'm certain they'll reach Loboche before us.

We manage to cut back down toward Pheriche right above the town, and have to search around a little to find an appropriate place to reenter, as Meenakshi points out that cutting through a yak pasture might not sit well with its owners.

We pass by an utterly filthy outhouse, perhaps the worst we've encountered on the trail so far, but manage to get to the Himalayan Rescue Association building by mid-afternoon, under a still misty but not cold sky.

MYSTERIOUS NAMCHE

*One of the most amazing towns in the world is Namche Bazaar,
the Sherpa capital and center of commerce and culture in the
Khumbu. Traders from Kathmandu and Tibet converge on
Namche weekly to sell goods at the town's famous market.*

NAMCHE SELFIE

We are relieved to reach Namche, where we'd spend two days acclimating.

AIRPORT IN THE CLOUDS

A plane lands at Tenzing-Hillary Airport in Lukla. At 9,383 feet, the airport is considered one of the most dangerous in the world. It's also the starting point for most treks to Base Camp.

SUNRISE LODGE

Marigolds flood the courtyard of the Sunrise Lodge, a tea house and accommodation deep in the Khumbu Valley.

MEHNDI CELEBRATION

On the day before the wedding, mehndi or henna, was applied to the bride's hands. Look for the names of the bride and groom.

NEPALI WEDDING

Meenakshi flashes a smile at the photographer during our wedding ceremony. Me? I'm just trying to concentrate and not flub things up!

CITY TRAFFIC MADNESS

The chaos of Kathmandu's crowded streets can be daunting to a Westerner.

THE AUTHOR'S NEW FAMILY

*My new brother-in-law Sandeep, mother-in-law
Rita, Meenakshi and father-in-law Kiran.*

THE GLACIER

We pause for a photo in front of the Khumbu Glacier which pours down off Mt. Everest. We'd now follow the glacier to Base Camp and to our mountain, Kala Patthar.

GRAND TREK

Meenakshi rounds a turn, heading toward Base Camp, with the flanks of Mt. Everest dominating the hike.

BASE CAMP

A moment of joy and release at the giant boulder at the original Base Camp.

A QUIET MOMENT

*I'm able to sneak down off the Base Camp plateau to explore
the giant ice seracs near the Khumbu Icefall.*

GRAND VIEW

From our perch atop Kala Patthar, the North Face of Mt. Everest (center) shimmers. To the right is Everest's sister mountain, Nuptse.

DANCING MONKS

The monks at Tengboche Monastery perform a sacred dance at the yearly Mani Rimdu Festival.

FRESH VEGETABLES

Cabbage fields line the trail near the Milk River. Fresh vegetables, grown right in the yards of the lodges, are one of the primary foods in the region.

PEACEFUL YAK

A shaggy yak grazes peacefully high above Namche Bazaar, waiting for its herder to give the command to head into town.

The HRA is a British-created and mostly British-run nonprofit hospital established in the early 1970s with the idea of reducing the number of Everest casualties through high-altitude education and training.

The post is a long one-story stone building, clean and well-funded, and is being operated by two British female volunteer doctors when we stop in. In 1973, an American national, Dr. John Skow, was tramping around Nepal on assignment with the Peace Corps when he noticed the alarming rate of people dying from altitude sickness. Upon returning to Britain, he somehow managed to convince a handful of trekking organizations to put up the money to create the HRA. And now, the place has its hands full. In 1973, fewer than 14,000 trekkers came to Nepal. Ten years later that number had jumped to 50,000. Now, three times that many tramp around the mountains each year. This year has been particularly bad for .the British doctors, with dozens of sick or injured trekkers coming in this season alone. When weather closes Lukla airport, guides and trekking groups tend to force-march their clients, oftentimes straight into the HRA suffering from altitude sickness. The irony is that people getting sick and needing rescue by the HRA most often come from the trekking groups that funded the place to begin with.

Now, aside from a daily lecture on altitude sickness held in the HRA's solarium, the place works mainly as an emergency room, mostly free of charge for locals, but not for trekkers. Oh, and they sell cool stuff as well! Patches, fleece scarves and sweaters and T-shirts are all on sale for fairly reasonable prices, at least by Western standards. I buy an HRA sweater for 750 rupees and wear that sucker for the next five days straight.

In a courtyard outside the HRA is a two-meter-high sculpture called "Broken Whole." Constructed to commemorate the 50th anniversary of Hillary and Tenzing's climb, the memorial sculpture was designed by British artist Oliver Barrett and carried to the site in eleven pieces by porters.

The sculpture is a polished stainless steel cone, split in two down the center. You can walk between the two halves, which are inscribed with the names of all who have perished on the Nepalese slopes of Everest. When the sculpture was erected, 174 climbers had died.

That number is now up to about 215, and about 65 percent of the names etched into the steel are Nepali.

The sculpture is completely out of place in this setting, and strange and moving at the same time. Meenakshi and I walk through the cones and run our fingers over the names. I touch the names of George Mallory and Pasang Llamu Sherpa and Scott Fischer. We're going there tomorrow, to the place where they all died.

It's getting on toward dark now, and we need some supplies, in particular toilet paper and yak cheese. We noticed the first for sale at a tiny bodega on the way to the HRA. Stacks of colorful toilet paper are on display right out in front, and I buy a roll to tide us over for the next few days. The cost is 450 rupees, more than half the cost of my fleece.

Meena asks the owner if he has any yak cheese, and after a spirited discussion with someone in the back, an enormous cheese wheel of the stuff is produced. He cuts us a piece the size of a cake wedge, then cuts that piece up into bite-sized morsels and bags it all up.

This is the real thing, tangy and stinky and filling, fresh from the animal and not sold to trekkers unless they ask. We will live off this hunk of cheese for the next week. Technically, since yaks are males and naks are females, the cheese is properly referred to as nak cheese, but hardly any Westerner follows the protocol.

With snacks at our side, we walk all the way out to the edge of town, facing our trail for the next day. The setting sun warms our backs and burns the mist off the ridges around us, and we lay out on some rocks with the specific idea in our heads that we'll be the welcoming committee for trekkers coming to town. The Pheriche Valley is miles long and any trekker coming into town would be able to see Pheriche from very far away. What a relief it must be to finally arrive!

So we lay out our cheese and crackers, make ourselves comfortable and wait. The afternoon is mild and we are feeling strong and happy and confident. We take pictures of the peaks. I pore over my maps to search for the proper names of these giants, and Meenakshi leans back and soaks in the sun.

The first woman to enter town is Australian. She is alone and tired. We have seen her coming from quite a distance.

"Hello," we both say chipperly. "Welcome to town! You made it!"
The woman is so confused it's funny.

She cocks her head. "I'm sorry, do I know you?"

"We're the welcoming committee," Meena says.

She stares at us.

"You don't know us," I say. "We just wanted to say hello!"

"Oh! Well, thank you."

As it turns out the woman is staying in our lodge tonight. Later, after dinner, the evening sky clears and a group of us pad outside to watch Awi Peak at the end of the valley light up bright white in the brilliant starlight. I loan my tiny tripod to Karlie, the young solo trekker from Ireland, and a friend, and they spend twenty minutes perfecting the exposure on their camera for a picture, Karlie counting the Mississippis while her friend holds the gadget still.

It will be over a month before that picture is emailed to me, and I'm still in awe of its beauty, in part because the shot is so clear, but mostly because it remains a memory for us of that amazing evening of peace and contentment.

Tomorrow we will reach the Khumbu Glacier. Or so we think.

Chapter 9

~

We Are Surrounded!

We have a lot of miles and 1000 feet in elevation to cover to Loboche, so we leave early again after a small breakfast of bread and a fried egg.

We're eating lighter now to keep our stomachs calm. A couple days ago, around Tengboche, we saw a porter carrying raw pork flank in his dirty basket, unwrapped, exposed to the elements for at least a day, red and soft and streaky. We decided to give up meat for the remainder of the trip.

We reluctantly bid our lodge-keepers goodbye, with the promise that we'll stop here on the way back as well.

The number for the day is daunting: 2,198. That's the difference in elevation between us and Loboche and it's all up. Trekking from 13,910 feet to 16,108 feet will be difficult.

Still, the morning is brilliant and clear. With only the hint of wispy mist swirling amid the high peaks, and a bright blue sky to greet us, we put on our shades, head through town and begin our trek through the valley that's been our home for two days.

We are well beyond trees now. Slight scrub pops up here and there, and we spot moss and rock algae from the nearby Loboche River. The valley is crisscrossed with deep ruts from the decades of yak trains and trekkers. We pick one trail and try to keep to it, but it doesn't matter much. All the trails go to the same place. Miles in front of us, the valley abruptly ends at the terminal moraine of the Khumbu Glacier.

For now, we walk slowly, taking our time to enjoy the high mountains that pierce the mist like white knives.

The valley is a raw, unrelenting and barren place, and it's the most beautiful hiking I've ever done. A dozen 20,000-foot peaks surround us, the river roars white, yak bells and the whistles of por-ters provide background music, and teams of climbers of all nation-alities pass us by, greeting us with "bonjour" and "good day" and "dzien dobry" and "namasta" and "hola."

We navigate a series of drainages that come down off the valley walls, and the trekking is tricky going through some mud, skip-ping around and over stones. The water is perfectly clear, nearly invisible. We pass some stone cairns that mark various yak herd paths. Multicolored flags jut up from the points and look like Native American feather monuments as they flutter under the peaks.

It's peaceful walking.

Midway through the valley, as the Loboche begins to widen toward the glaciers, sits the summer village of Tsambur, a seasonal yak shepherds' town sometimes referred to as a goth. It's mostly empty now; the herders are out working for trekkers, their yaks earning their keeps. We wander quietly through the village, its stone huts right up against the path, painted and weathered doors bolted and windows boarded up. I see smoke coming up from one tiny stone hut far off the main path, but no signs of life. Perhaps the owner has made his home available for passing porters during the trekking season.

The buildings are stone, the path is stone, the walls and gates are stone—stone from the earth and stone from the mountains. We walk through a valley of rock, at our feet and thousands of feet above us.

Through the morning we are accompanied by 21,463-foot Taboche and 21,129-foot Cholatse, sister peaks connected by a sharp ridge, both with curious histories.

In 1974, a French team led by Yannick Lord defied a ban on climbing Taboche and summited with a group that included jazz clarinetist Jean-Christian Michel. For his efforts, Lord was barred from Nepal for some time.

Cholatse, whose name literally means Lake Pass Peak, has an even more colorful pedigree in the distinction of being the last named peak climbed in the Himal. Mainly it's just hard. It's a stun-ning mountain with steep drops and narrow ridges of ice and snow. Commercial trekking companies haul clients up Everest every year. None have climbed Cholatse.

The first team to do it was American and consisted of two famous landscape photographers, leader Vern Clevenger and partner Galen Rowell. In 1982 they tackled the southwest ridge and described the climb as having some twenty pitches of difficult ice climbing.

The two mountains shimmer and shine in the brilliant sunlight, and with every step a new cliff, ice wall or crag is revealed. We walk for hours in the shadow of those two glorious peaks and they look different every time I lift up my head.

The Chola Glacier pours down off the east face of Cholatse, huge and thick, like chocolate and white syrup.

It takes us nearly three hours to get to the end of the valley, and we stop for a snack and to catch our breath before the next phase of our journey. In front of us the valley disintegrates into a series of options. To the south, Taboche and Cholatse seem to form an impenetrable wall of ice and rock, though we can see distinct trail ruts that appear to head straight up the ice walls.

To the west, trails cut wildly across the river outlet and disappear behind a tremendous ridge. This is the Cho La Pass, a challenging mountain pass that leads to the Goyko Lakes and is sometimes used as a loop to head back to Namche. The next time I'm here, I think, that's where I'll go.

But today, we turn north and begin the steep series of terraced climbs that will take us first to the tiny town of Dughla for lunch, then up and over the moraine and the glacier.

It's hard going, not steep but constant. The trail swings us up a couple hundred feet, around the long north ridge of the Pheriche Valley, and levels out somewhat on a deeply rutted plateau. Taboche's enormous flat north face is directly at our backs and the mountain, only a couple miles away, seems impossibly huge, a sun-blotting tower of shimmering ice and rock.

I step up a slight rise above the plateau, with much difficulty, to let Meenakshi take a bunch of pictures of me against the towering spires of Cholatse. I can barely breathe, and she takes a quick video of me walking as fast as I can along that ridge. It is not fast by any stretch of the imagination and I have to slow down when I feel the sharp, familiar pinprick of an altitude headache creep up on me. I've discovered that a few deep, meditative breaths usually alleviate the headache. I take a moment there so high in the sky to calm myself before continuing.

After a half hour on the plateau, we continue on the trail. It turns sharply toward the sound of rushing water and there it is, the terminal moraine of Everest's Khumbu Glacier.

Also called an end moraine, it marks the maximum advance of the glacier. It is at this point that all the debris that has accumulated has been pushed to the front end of the ice and dumped into a giant mound of rock and ice and earth.

The Khumbu's terminal moraine is spectacular, a tremendous natural buttress the size of one of New Hampshire's mountains. At its easternmost end, the glacier water has crashed through a thousand little crevices and pours down the moraine eventually leading to the Loboche. The water I dipped my hand in last week came from here—the Loboche empties into the Imja, which empties into the Milk.

The outwash from the glacier at this time of year is only five or six feet wide, but it roars like a freight train off the moraine and into the valley. The rocks around the outwash are scoured a blinding white.

On the other side of the wash and up a small rise is Dughla, really more a truck stop than a village proper.

We're already tired, even though it's only noon, and the high sun is relentless. We scramble down to the outwash, cross over on a sturdy-looking steel trestle bridge and then scramble back up a ledge to reach the village.

We're happy to be in Dughla, which we've also heard referred to as Thukla. We order two cups of noodles and some milk tea and look around for a place to people-watch and enjoy the sun in the courtyard of one of the two lodges in town. There is a wonderful stone wall that overlooks a beautiful view back down toward Pheriche, but we are dismayed to discover that a commercial trekking crew has dumped its gear on the stone seats and is eating loudly at an adjacent table.

Meenakshi does not care for this and makes her displeasure known by hauling two enormous packs off the seats, tossing them to the dusty ground, and plopping herself down to enjoy the view. A few heads from the group turn, but no one appears willing to make a fuss, and it's a good thing.

We have our seats, our views, our lunch, our sun and our mountains. We decide on the spot that this is where we'll stay tonight, using the afternoon to acclimate further, to rest and soak in the views.

I do some quick calculations in my head and determine that splitting this day into two halves will not affect our return flight. It does mean that the hike back will have to take four days instead of five, something I feel is doable.

So here we are, at 15,157 feet, at the very base of Mt. Everest's Khumbu Glacier. Meenakshi shakes off her heavy jacket and gloves, finds a plastic patio chair to lean back in, and turns her face to the sun.

"This is my beach day," she announces. And so it is!

With the whole afternoon before me, I consider my next steps. First, I secure us a room.

"With the best views!" I tell the bemused lodge owner, a very young Nepali with a DKNY T-shirt, jeans and rock-and-roll hair.

"Best room in lodge, sir!" he says, handing me a key as his friends laugh. He might be teasing me, but he does give us a wonderful room at the end of a long corridor, its one window pointed straight at Ama Dablam.

I spread out our bags and gear, wash my face and brush my teeth in the freezing cold water at the common sink down the hall. Then I go outside to explore a little bit.

Besides the two lodges, there is one snack store selling most of the typical Coke and Mars bar offerings. Here, though, a woman is selling colorful handmade alpine hats. We've been looking for a certain type of hat for Meena, with a row of mohawk-like threads down the middle.

I ask the storekeeper if they sell those, but she just shakes her head sadly and points. On a bench, watching over the boys who run the lodge, is an old, plump woman, obviously their grandmother. She is wearing the mohawk hat.

"One left," says the woman behind the counter. "But it's hers."

The old woman jokes loudly with the boys as they jostle and punch each other in the arm in the courtyard. She gives some instructions to another man, perhaps her own son, who runs off into the lodge. She is the mistress of this village, and I decide she should keep her hat.

So, with the moraine so close, and with time on my hands and still no sign of the daily afternoon showers, I decide to explore the glacier outwash.

First I climb up on a ridge above the lodge and take some pictures, and I smile when I see Meenakshi down at the lodge taking pictures of me. I sit up on that rise for a while, watching the mist and clouds float around Ama and Thamserku and Kangtanga.

I scramble back down to the bridge and rock-hop up the outwash. Higher and higher up the moraine I go until my altimeter reads 15,500 feet. I'm alone up here, above the lodge and the trail. I'm alone, playing in Mt. Everest's runoff, the clear water running under my feet, my breath coming in fits and starts, but feeling strong. The runoff cascades down from a hundred points in the moraine, but all of it channels into one main huge groove cut out of the earth. Instead of going back the way I came, I scout out a wall that I can scramble up, hoping to loop back down to the lodge from a different route.

The outwash walls on the lodge side are eight or ten feet high in some places, and I shimmy my way up the gravelly, eroded wall and get under the lip of the outwash rut.

It's a tricky climb, and as I maneuver up and out of the rut, a rock shifts under my foot. In my mind, I imagine myself falling backward into the wash, sucked down by the current, slipping past the lodge where my dinner is being made, under the bridge I crossed and down into the valley below, where I would be lost in minutes. And perhaps little Chori Tenzing, the girl who entertained us the evening before, would see my red jacket passing by in the current and be the only witness to my demise and not even know it.

I swallow hard, focus on my footing, and pull myself up and out of the outwash and onto hard land.

I'm in a place where there is no mercy, where the most beautiful things are also the most unforgiving.

It takes me a while to catch my breath, and I suddenly no longer wish to be by myself. I head back at a quick pace to where Meenakshi waits.

Chapter 10
—
The Glacier

We barely get out of there with our lives!

Actually it's more funny than dangerous.

Last night, one of the very young Nepali lodge keepers nearly burned the place down trying to show off. A crew of porters had taken over the yak dung stove in the common room and was happily buzzed on Chang. The young man was obviously trying to earn some machismo points with them.

Meenakshi and I watched over our dinner of rice and soup as the young man dumped a load of dung into the stove, then squirted what seemed like a whole container of either lighter fluid or straight-up gasoline onto it. Streaks of the stuff got on the stove, on his hands and on the floor.

We hardly had time to exchange a horrified glance before the boy lit a piece of paper and tried to drop it into the stove.

Whooosh! A fireball exploded out of the stove, sending the boy and half the porters scrambling for cover. Fortunately nothing caught on fire and only the boy's ego and maybe his eyebrows were singed as the porters themselves all exploded, but in laughter. Even Meena and I laughed and the boy seemed to take the teasing well. I think everyone was just relieved the whole place didn't go up!

Today we are up and out early once again, as there is no longer any guarantee of spaces in Loboche. Like the day before, our hope is to get there before noon and spend the afternoon acclimating and exploring the town.

But the morning seems to happen in slow motion as we struggle up the Khumbu's moraine. It's hard work, and we have little breath left for the breathtaking views to take.

Our elevation today will be gained in the morning climb up the moraine, nearly 1,000 feet all at once, up to 16,100 feet. It's too daunting to think much about. So far, our stomachs have been fine, though we are being careful what we eat. Occasional sharp headaches like pinpricks at the base of my skull will flare, but slowing down and taking a few deep breaths mostly clears that up.

The trail winds its way up the moraine in moderate switchbacks and we manage to get about halfway up before the regular trail traffic begins to appear.

Porters half our size with twice our loads and shorter than Meenakshi zoom by us like we are standing still. The regular yak trains give us excuses to stop and catch our breath. Last night, from atop the small plateau above Dughla, it seemed impossible that views could get much better, but up here they do. We turn around often to take in the whole Pheriche Valley, long and deep, the direct sunlight turning the valley floor silver and gold.

After about two hours, a col in the top of the rise comes into view, and we follow a cairn gateway up onto the edge of the moraine, more than 16,000 feet above sea level. And though I've read about it in the tour books, what we enter is stunning and humbling.

At the top of the Khumbu Glacier's terminal moraine exists a memorial garden to all the climbers taken by Everest. Dozens of chortens, stupas and rock piles of various heights and construction dot the immense plateau.

Anyone hiking to Base Camp or climbing Mt. Everest from the south must pass through this garden, in essence the highest cemetery on the planet, a place of extreme emotional impact. Thousands of prayer flags, some new, some decades old, flutter over and around the memorials. Some have plaques and inscriptions and are well kept up; some are ancient piles of rocks, crumbling and returning to the Earth.

Meenakshi and I separate and wander without direction through the memorials. There is nothing to say. I run my hand over the rocks, warm in the sun, thinking about all the people who attained this ridge on their way to Everest, as we have, and never came back down.

Lost in my thoughts, I stumble upon the chorten dedicated to Scott Fischer. For the past week, as I have moved through this beautiful country, I have been surrounded by evidence of its harsher potential, but only now does the full impact of this trip, of where I am, of all those who came before me, become fully realized.

I draw a bare finger over the gold plaque fastened to the side of the rocks:

IN MEMORY OF
SCOTT EUGENE FISCHER
WHO DIED ON MT. EVEREST
MAY 11, 1996
HIS SPIRIT LIVES ON

I do not idolize Fischer. His death on Everest more than fifteen years ago was not glamorous or romantic. Fischer died in one of the worst single-day tragedy in climbing history on Mt. Everest. As the owner of Mountain Madness, an adventure company that foolishly guaranteed successful summits to its clients, Fischer more than anyone had, over the years, become the poster child of the tragic consequences of commercialism in the Khumbu.

Fischer had once told a reporter that he had Everest figured out. He was wrong.

Many books have been written about that day, the most famous being Jon Krakauer's *Into Thin Air*. That's a book I read while living in New Jersey, before taking one step into the White Mountains, before attempting Mt. Rainier, before hiking across England, before summiting Guadalupe in Texas or Humphreys in Arizona or Harney in South Dakota. It is the book that made me wonder what all this was about, what could cause so many people to undergo so much suffering to simply stand atop a pile of rocks for five minutes.

Now I knew. And now I was here. My God, I'm here.

Meenakshi comes up behind me and we stand there quietly for a minute. I hand her our good camera.

"This is Scott Fischer," I say. "Can you take our picture?"

After a while we leave this place of memories, but only after Meenakshi points to a wide flat rock in the middle of all the ghosts. On this rock, someone has constructed an outline of a heart with pebbles and stones. Is it an expression of love amid all this death? Is it its own memorial constructed by someone who lost a loved one here? I think of it as a sign of hope, and maybe luck—a reminder that beauty and horror can coexist here, and often do.

The plateau at the top of the moraine is a half mile long. We move slowly around a slight curve, trying to absorb the knowledge that we are standing on the tip of the glacier, Everest's glacier.

All those thoughts drain out of my head, though, as we climb up a slight rise and a familiar shape appears far in the distance. Pumori. It's Pumori!

The mountain is a perfect triangle, a cone of white towering above the ridge at the far end of the glacier, a distinct waymarker of the border between Nepal and Tibet. But more importantly for us, our destination. Kala Patthar, sits at the foot of Pumori. It's the end. We can see it now.

Once again Meenakshi and I stop in the trail and gawk. We do a lot of that now, stopping and looking. "Pumori," I mumble. "Kala is there, that ridge."

I point out the distinct ridge that leads to a bump under the shimmering Pumori. We're still ten miles away.

"That's Kala Patthar?" Meenakshi asks.

"Yeah."

The day is warm and blue, and the trail smells sweetly of a particular type of clove that locals claim has "medicinal" benefits.

Two weeks ago I stood with this woman on an altar in Kathmandu, with colors all around us, surrounded by incense and fire, with an out-of-control band playing happily and family and friends offering us their blessings. Now, I stand here at the edge of Nepal, the highest place on Earth, where the trail still smells like incense, the colors are still so bright it seems unreal and the music of the wind and water and yak bells plays.

How can this be my life?

The rest of the hike to Loboche is uneventful, if anyone in their right mind could call this place uneventful. We drop down to the glacier runoff and hug the eastern valley wall as we make our way toward Kala.

About a half hour outside of Loboche, a familiar face passes me by. "Oh hey! Remember me?"

"Lene!" And this time I do give him a quick hug. The hell with custom at this point.

Lene Oh is returning with his client. They summited Kala

Patthar but decided not to go for Base Camp—too far, too little time, too difficult.

We chat a little bit and once again Lene reads my mind and asks if we have anything booked for Loboche. We don't, of course.

"Eco-Lodge," he says. "Go right there, far end of town, they will have rooms. But hurry!"

Before Lene leaves I slip him 200 rupees. He resists at first, but then seems grateful. This odd little man with no connection to us, and nothing to gain, helped us twice now, and I was not going to let him go without helping back.

"Thank you, Lene, you've really been great."

"Oh no!" Lene Oh says. "I'm glad, I'm glad. Bye bye!"

He heads off, sure-footed and determined, his client stumbling along behind him, and I find myself feeling very sad to see him go.

It's a straight shot into the village now, and we can hear the tink, tink, tink of stone masons' hammers before we see the buildings. Apparently there is a building boom in Loboche as well.

It's been a long morning, and we are very high and very hungry. The Eco-Lodge is on the far side of town, a huge place, and fairly new, compared to the rest.

We beat the lunch crowd and discover happily that we have the common area to ourselves as a lone lodge keeper washes the floors. The place is tremendously clean and expansive for a trekkers' lodge and it turns out Lene Oh was right once again, but just barely. There is one room left, and it's expensive comparatively. But we gladly pay the 700 rupees and consider ourselves lucky to have found anything.

We have a quick lunch of noodles and split a very tasty grilled cheese sandwich before heading up to our room.

The Eco-Lodge is actually two buildings, and our room is at the very end of the second, connected by an outside flight of stairs that I suddenly find very hard to climb. It's still a new and disconcerting experience for us to be out of breath after ten stairs.

Our room is huge and has wall-to-wall carpeting. It could fit a half dozen people compared to the last few places we've stayed. But we're glad to be here and I take some time to wash up, brush my teeth and scrub a little Vaseline into my beard and scalp. My skin is very dry and has begun to blister and chip in some places.

We rest for a while, then decide, with the whole afternoon left, to take a short acclimatization hike up to an Italian Research Center along the trail to Gorak Shep, our destination for tomorrow.

As usual, an afternoon haze has settled over the high peaks as we set out, but the day is still reasonably warm and our day packs make the going much easier. The center is about two miles up the trail, near Loboche Glacier, and we take our time, moving slowly over the ups and downs of the glacier valley.

To our left, the flanks of Loboche rise up in a series of ridges and hills. To our right, the runoff of the Khumbu Glacier creates a mini-valley, giving trekkers enough space to walk. The main part of the glacier is on the other side of a rocky berm, three or four stories over our heads.

My stomach feels slightly unsettled as we walk, a feeling similar to a cramp, but generally we feel strong. So far, we have managed to avoid any negative effects of altitude. Perhaps the two-a-day Pepto Bismol tablets have helped.

We hike along happily, Mera Peak gleaming in and out of clouds to the east, until we reach a faint crossroads in the trail. The intersection to the center would be easy to miss if not for there being a couple tents set up alongside the trail, perhaps by interns or researchers at the center. We hang a left, and the trail thins into a deeply carved slot valley, then opens up into a wide muddy basin at the foot of Loboche Glacier. And as we come around a final curve, we see the top of the center, a solar-paneled pyramid, poking up from the rocks.

"It's like a spaceship has landed!" Meenakshi says.

It's so strange to see this modern building here, two week's walk from any road and only a few hours from Base Camp. The pyramid shines like a blue-glass beacon, reflecting the surrounding rocks and mountains in its bug-like multi-eyes.

The center is a research facility, doing weather broadcasting as well as high-altitude experiments, and hosting scientists from all over the world in three-month programs. But like most institutions in this country, it got its start in a very different way.

In the late 1980s an American team of climbers, after summitting K2, claimed that it, not Everest, was actually the highest peak in the world. As you can imagine, this did not sit well with the Brits, as they did not want Hillary's accomplishment to be overshadowed by Americans. So, with the help of the Italians, who were in the middle of some early experiments with Global Positioning Systems (GPS), they set about building a research center for the sole purpose of accurately measuring the two peaks.

The official name of the facility is Ev-K2-CNR (CNR after the Italian research group). Its website is www.evk2cnr.org.

And so, one of the most modern scientific research centers in the world was built at high cost and much labor, in the middle of nowhere, to prove that Americans were full of shit.

None of this matters to us, of course, as we stretch out on a little rise near the center and enjoy a yak cheese snack, because this place is extraordinary. It's far enough off the trekking track that the hiker flow is minimal. The center is surrounded by peaks on three sides and a glacier on the fourth.

As we sit and relax, we hear the low rumble of an avalanche someplace high in the mist on Loboche. I do not use this term often, or loosely, but this place is magical.

There are no scientists here now, but a pleasant Nepali caretaker asks if we'd like a tour, and we eagerly accept. He takes us into the main lab, a conference room, a computer center and a variety of other rooms with machines and beakers and flashing buttons.

It's all interesting, but what I really want to see is where they live. I pretend to need to go to the bathroom, and my ruse works as the man leads me down a below-ground staircase into the living quarters and lets me go in alone.

I am drawn like a magnet to the toilet—completely Western in style, and it flushes! They even have a shower and hot water. I take off my hat, fill my cupped hands with hot tap water and splash it on my face and head. I have no clue how a flush toilet and hot running water can exist up here. I imagine people much smarter about such things, like Meenakshi for example, could tell me, but I don't want to know. For now, it's a tiny Khumbu miracle and it feels wonderful.

Up to two dozen scientists and researchers can live here at any one time, and they have comfortable-looking bunk beds, a large kitchen area with a sink, and a comfortable recreation room with some books and board games. I don't see a television but I bet there's one someplace around here.

After about ten minutes, not wanting to make our host suspicious, I take my leave, and Meenakshi and I head back to Loboche for the evening.

It's getting on in the afternoon now, and I'm thrilled when I see Jim's crew on the trail. They are one day ahead of us, but they look pretty ragged. One of their number has already dropped out and they are pushing hard now, with the intent of attempting Kala Patthar the next day. It looks like they will have to skip Base Camp.

I wish them good luck and breathe a sigh of relief that we are able to keep our own schedule and come and go as we please.

Back in Loboche, as the sun sets and a cold rain tracks up the valley, we find ourselves back in the Eco-Lodge fighting for space in the now very crowded common room. It turns out the Eco-Lodge is popular with the commercial hiking groups, and solo trekkers like ourselves are given little consideration when compared to the overwhelming amount of money a lodge keeper can make from a big organized tour. That night, we are pushed to a corner by the presence of Exodus, the commercial trekking equivalent of Wal-Mart.

Trek with Exodus and you get guaranteed rooms, meals and hot tea and cookies waiting for you when you arrive in town, solar-panel-heated water and a small army of porters and guides to cater to your every whim. You also get a hefty price tag—a trek like this could cost upwards of $5,000.

By comparison, Meenakshi and I will have spent about $250 each, except for airfare.

We grumble but slide over and make way for the loud, rude groups. We're just happy we have a room.

After another meal of soup and momos we head for bed. The time has come. Tomorrow, we will set out for Gorak Shep, the last village on the line, at the base of Kala Patthar. Tomorrow afternoon, we'll attempt to push past Gorak Shep for a side trip to Base Camp.

We are exhausted and dirty, but our spirits are high and our stomachs are relatively strong. We have driven ourselves for the past year, training hard. Meenakshi and I sacrificed a lot of time and energy to get here, to make this final push, to be where we were right now. The next forty-eight hours will tell the tale.

Kala Patthar waits ahead.

Before bed, I step outside one final time to check the weather and am horrified to discover how hard the snow is blowing down. Just outside the door, a giant yak, coated white and barely recognizable under the snow, shakes its bells like laughter.

Chapter 11

~

Dead Ravens

Many years ago, Meenakshi and I climbed Mt. Jefferson in New Hampshire. We had only known each other for a little while, had just started properly dating, and had only climbed one mountain before—Mt. Lafayette on a picture perfect bluebird day.

Mt. Jefferson was different. It was summer but the weather was terrible, real hypothermia-inducing raw weather. I had not led many climbs before this one, and I guess I was showing off a little, or trying to.

We reached tree line and the wind and rain came at us like a freight train, sideways and relentless. But we had Gore-Tex and we pushed on. It got cold, then colder, then more windy. We tagged the summit in howling rain and near zero visibility and decided to descend down a different trail, called The Link, because we were too afraid of backtracking down the steep and, in this weather, dangerous, Caps Ridge Trail.

It was hell—eroded roots, crumbling dirt, washed-out rocks and near vertical drops. There were times when we had to swing from tree branch to tree branch to avoid pitching down the slope. And all through this, the rain and cold continued. To call it a character-builder would be generous. By the end we were sniping at each other, soaking wet and just about as exhausted as we've ever been on a hike.

It was a hike and a route that, ten years later, I would not do, alone or with anyone. Today, if faced with those conditions, I would turn back.

But we did it, and later, after our muscles and egos healed, we joked about it. It became a Story in our lives, a mutual experience that despite the difficulty did not push us apart, but drew us together.

It's a hike that serves as a waymark in our adventures.

"Well," we say, "at least it's not as hard as Mt. Jefferson." And we laugh.

I think of this story on the morning of our attempt to reach Everest Base Camp because I need to draw on the memory for strength. I am alone, and I am uneasy.

We have made a mutual decision on this ninth day of our trek to split up, breaking the first rule of climbing. I agonized over it last night as Meenakshi and I discussed our strategy for this morning.

The facts were plain: If we did not get to Gorak Shep by 9:00 or 9:30 a.m. today, we might very well find ourselves, at best, sleeping on a cold floor, or, at worst, having to turn around and go all the way back to Loboche. Our side trek to Base Camp, from Gorak Shep, needs to be accomplished early enough today so that we have time to recover and prepare in order to tackle Kala tomorrow.

We were both beat, but Meenakshi had more left in her gas tank than I did. She carried less in her pack, and we both knew that she could get to Gorak Shep faster than me, likely by forty-five minutes or more.

So, before six a.m., we passed on breakfast, gobbled down piles of crackers and cheese and stepped outside into the snow and haze to begin the trek to our final town. Just outside of Loboche, as the valley trail headed into the Khumbu toward Everest, I went over last-minute instructions. *Don't be afraid to use the map or ask for directions. You're going to be moving faster than you're used to, so drink more water than you normally would. Take breaks.*

Then I kissed her, and she moved off into the mist.

It was an interesting feeling, terror mixing with pride. She is so strong, and we'd been doing this sort of thing for so long. I knew in my heart that this was the right decision for the moment. But watching the mist swallow Meenakshi, and then setting out alone, was one of the most difficult moments of the trip for me.

The trail to Gorak Shep is straightforward enough—I hug the inner valley of the Khumbu Glacier for the first few miles, pass by the Italian Research Center we reached yesterday, climb up to the moraine level of the Khumbu—and then it gets tricky. Three

glaciers, the Khumbu, the Changri Shar and the Changri Nup, converge in a giant intersection right before the village and right at the
base of Kala Patthar. The final mile is up and down over this three-
way glacier headwall at 17,000 feet.

I am relieved to discover that the trail is well worn. It would be
nearly impossible for me, short of a mental breakdown, to miss and
take a wrong turn. Plus, after about thirty minutes I am virtually surrounded by trekkers, both going up and coming down. All through
the morning trek I'm distracted by mental calculations of where
Meena might be. I imagine what the terrain might have looked like
thirty minutes, forty-five minutes, one hour before I set foot here.
Did she have a hard time finding the trail?

The morning is full of snow and mist. After the cutoff to the
research center, I move up and around a slight rise to a long wide
rocky flat area a half mile long that seems to shoot straight up a
crumbly hill that I assume is the beginning of the glacier intersection.

Then, something happens. I begin to see ridges through the mist,
high at first, then lower down. Slivers of blue begin to peek around
corners and long bands of sun punch through the clouds like lasers
highlighting strips on the ground here and there.

I stop to gulp down some water and catch my breath, and as I
stand there the remaining mist lifts like a miracle and Pumori reveals
itself above the ridge, a towering, impossible apparition.

It is awesome and startling—6,000 feet of Pumori's perfectly
shaped triangular summit cone floats above the ridge, above the
clouds. The trekkers around me stop and stare. We all stare. There
is no sound. We are less than five miles from this 25,000-foot mountain and it is perfect. It is astounding.

Pumori, Everest's Daughter, rising up like that out of the mist
will become my defining moment of this trip, the single second of
overwhelming smallness and humility that surges up my spine. I
have never seen anything like it. I can't imagine ever seeing anything
like it again.

I shake off my terror and awe and start taking pictures, praying
that Meenakshi is someplace where she can see this, where we can
be apart yet share this experience later.

The final climb up to the glacier intersection takes an hour, and I move slowly, zigzagging up the rise like my legs are filled with lead. I'm bolstered by the magnet of Pumori, and every step pulls me closer to its gravity.

At the top of the rise, I see the Khumbu Glacier and the giant Changris pouring down from either side of Changri Peak, pouring down from Tibet. I begin the daunting final pull over the three moraines, and it's hard going, because I can feel the altitude like invisible claws digging into my calves and pushing on my shoulders, and also because the trail here is hard. The moraines are rocks and rubble and the trail tries to hug the outside edge of the ridge closest to the Khumbu, but sometimes it darts down to a runoff before climbing back to the outside.

I stop many times to take pictures and to suck wind. But I am surrounded by massive peaks, long flowing glaciers and sky so blue it seems oversaturated. *How can sky be this blue?* I wonder. My mind tries to get around my surroundings, but it's some kind of visual overload. There is nothing in my memory to hold onto, to put what I'm seeing in context, and I feel like a cup that is overflowing.

I have to shake my head. I stand at a turn in the trail overlooking the glacier and shout "Phew!" and "Wow!" Saying what I'm thinking seems to take the edge off and I settle my head and move on.

After a few more twists and turns and ups and downs, just when I think I can stand the uncertainty no more, I see Gorak Shep and my heart soars. I want to run down to this unreal place, this last outpost that seems like it's at the end of the universe.

Gorak Shep, the original Base Camp. The place where Mallory and Hillary lived as they prepared for Everest. Gorak Shep is a collection of stone and tin huts, pointed this way and that at the foot of a dry glacier lake bed at nearly 17,000 feet.

The name means Dead Ravens, and I laugh out loud as I trot down a slight hill into town.

Meenakshi is waiting for me outside, near the edge of town, and I feel delirious relief and happiness in seeing her and in being here, near the end of our journey, finally.

We embrace and she's all grins. It's ten a.m. She beat me to the town by nearly an hour, in part by keeping pace with a group of Australian boys. Leave it to Meena's competitive nature to propel her. She managed to book the last open space in town, two bunks side by side in a dorm-style room.

I dump my gear, break out my down pants and jacket, and we scramble inside the lodge to grab lunch and prepare for an afternoon trek to Everest Base Camp.

The sun is out, but it's cold here and the lodge stove is not fired up yet, so we find a corner and squeeze together in the sun over grilled cheese sandwiches and tomato soup. We're tired and our stomachs are queasy, but our plan is solid. The weather is holding, and we have the whole afternoon.

Base Camp is three long miles away and 700 more feet above us, but this is our chance. We can visit Base Camp today, and then take our shot at Kala Patthar tomorrow.

From where we sit, Kala looks much, much taller than it did hours earlier in the shadow of Pumori. It's a giant brown mound of rock and dirt, 1,500 feet straight up. I take my sunglasses off and look up at this mountain that we have struggled and sacrificed the past year to reach. It is a tower of menace, a high, frightening lump of ice, a giant ominous wedding cake, complete with three tiers and a triple summit that will challenge us tomorrow. I turn away. I need to focus now on Base Camp. One challenge at a time.

We lay out our bags and prepare our bunks for our return, not knowing exactly when that return will be. In our day packs we carry water, headlamps, one extra layer and some first aid and emergency supplies. I carry Cindy's memory flag rolled up in my jacket. We check our batteries—I shove some extras in my jacket pocket—and we are on our way.

First we must walk over the dry glacier lake bed, a place with an insane sporting history. It is the site of the annual Everest Marathon, the highest marathon in the world—from Gorak Shep to Namche. No, seriously, there is an annual Everest Marathon.

Also, for a former lake bed, the area is surprisingly flat and devoid of any rocks or stones. That's because in 2009 it was also the site of the highest field sporting event in the world, a cricket match between two 11-person teams of Brits. An advance crew of locals painstakingly cleared the area of rocks and debris so the playing area could be flat and the pitch set up.

We move through this surreal landscape and gain a small rise that will send us up and over the flat lake bed and onto the spine of the Khumbu, a rocky ridge that will run for nearly three miles to Base Camp.

The time is noon. We pause at a sign that announces "Way to Mt. Everest Base Camp." We both pose for a picture and my head is swimming.

We're here. This is it. Here we go.

Chapter 12

—

Base Camp

A long, aching groan fills the air. It sounds like something is coming up from the earth to swallow us. The groan is followed by a sharp crack—a thousand iron hammers hitting a thousand anvils.

The glacier moves like a living thing, a constantly writhing eight-mile snake made of ice and rocks. It makes thunder.

The Khumbu is alive, and we are tiny, walking on its narrow spine, a good half mile up slope from the ice. It's like walking on a sleeping monster. A minuscule shift in the ice someplace out of sight creates massive shifts above and that energy explodes with the force of an earthquake. Here on this ridge, we can feel the glacier move and hear it crack, and it makes us want to move faster, to avoid angering it. But we can't. In fact, we can barely move at all. We are at 17,000 feet and ascending and it's like walking in glue.

The three-mile hike from Gorak Shep to Base Camp is not technical. It should not be difficult under normal circumstances. But this place is far from anything that we would ever call normal. We are so far beyond our comfort zone. We are specks floating on the top of the world. We are nothing here, we are all we have.

I am beyond words. Meenakshi and I share little because we can't afford the energy, but we can feel it, the power of this place.

The glacier speaks again and we stop to listen. Someplace from high on Nuptse (or on the other side, or in Tibet for all we know) a miles-wide crevasse opens and an avalanche comes tumbling down and we can feel the rumble in our bones and under our feet. We scan the ridges for the plumes of white but can see none.

I am trying to understand my place here. In between the upset stomach, the shifting weather, the porters coming and going, I work hard to be in the moment, to attain some level of mindfulness, as

Buddhists would say. The trail and the rocks and the ice and the air are the physical that is here. My amazing wife and our past and future, and the history of all who have come and all who will come swirl in my mind.

Irvine. Mallory. Norgay. Tabei. Messner. Krakauer. Arnot. Viesturs. We walk in their footsteps now. Tomorrow it will be our footsteps that those who come will follow. We follow history, we make history.

There is no yesterday, there is no today. There is now. And right now, we move silently through the swirling snowflakes, watching our time, watching our steps and trying to watch the giant mountains all around us.

A large commercial trekking group moves past us, fast, and several of their number are in distress. Meenakshi overhears a porter asking one young woman over and over if she'd like to go back.

"No, no, no," she says again and again. Being this close, it feels like it would be far more difficult to turn around than to continue even if continuing means pain and sickness.

We move on, dizzy, oxygen-deprived, sweating and freezing in turns. It is hard work, I must confess. There are two Base Camps, the old and the new. The new is empty for the season, no bakery, no mess tents. Just rocks, 2K farther along than the old. The old is where people are going.

After a series of twists around long ridge lines we come to a long straightaway, and we can see it now, tiny ant-like forms scurrying about in a high flattish region near the icefall. It seems impossibly far away. Distance is deceiving here. A mile of space, surrounded by the enormity of the Himal, appears to have no end, to be an illusion. After an unknowable amount of time, we see that the trail swoops down off the spine, into a glacier gully, then back up to the edge of the icefall where Base Camp waits, where a dozen or more trekkers appear to be congregating.

It's late in the afternoon by the time we begin our final approach, dropping off the ridge and down into the mouth of the Khumbu. We are in the headwaters now. The Khumbu forms a giant cirque, surrounded on three sides by Everest's icefall to our right, Pumori at our backs and Khumbutse straight ahead, a smaller peak over which, someplace up high, is supposedly a pass to Tibet. It is too big to imagine.

Meenakshi climbs up out of the gully ahead of me, to take pictures of me coming up. Later she will tell me that this was the point where it became very real, where she understood that we were no longer on earth, but on shifting ice, dozens of feet deep.

I am surrounded by people, but I am alone. I savor these final steps, my breathing hoarse and raw, like an animal's. My poles dig roughly into the gravel and ice and I pause near the top to see Meenakshi looking down at me, waving slowly with one hand, making a video with the other. I wave back.

In a few minutes I join her and the two of us stride the final few feet together to Base Camp. There is a refrigerator-sized boulder there, with the doodles and scribbles of generations of trekkers.

Base Camp. Base Camp. Base Camp . . .

It is bedlam. There are easily three dozen people here, and most of them are crying, or shouting, or both. Couples and men and women embrace and slap each other on the back. Someone has brought a flask of something, and he lifts it in the air toward the mountain and tips it to his mouth. Porters and trekkers unfurl flags of different countries and organizations in front of the rock. To my left, the young woman we saw earlier collapses and begins to weep, shaking and moaning. Her friends kneel down and put their arms around her, forming a huddle, and they all cry together.

It is a place of enormous and raw emotion. That rock is like a valve, letting out the pent up struggle of the people who have worked so hard to get here.

Meenakshi and I hug and for a few moments we are alone. We move inward to each other, a silent profound few seconds of personal joy. I hand her the good camera, and move to the rock, and bend over and kiss it, feeling its grainy, cold skin against my lips.

I hand the camera to one of the boys from Australia Meena followed earlier, and she and I crouch down in front of the rock. He takes a couple pictures, but suddenly I feel Meena grab me around the shoulders and pull me to her.

"This is my honeymoon!" she cries. We laugh and I raise my fist in jubilation and we are caught on camera like that, in a moment of unplanned posing.

After we untangle, Meena wanders over to a small open area where some Himalayan Ravens are buzzing about. They hop around tamely and she offers some trail mix, which they shyly peck out of her gloved hands. It's amazing that there are living creatures here.

Almost in a daze, I shuffle down off the Base Camp plateau toward the icefall. Thousands of huge seracs, eight and ten and twelve feet high, shoot straight up off the ground and shimmer like daggers in the mist and swirling snow. I notice that I've been fooled by another misperception of distance. The icefall is really fifty yards away, beyond a large cliff-like glacier crevasse that, from here anyway, I can't cross.

I suddenly feel so tired, and my legs just give out and I don't fight it. I sit down on the ice facing the seracs and I cry—not a weeping wailing cry. I am just so tired, and I am sitting at the Khumbu Icefall and my body does not have the energy to block them, so the tears just run down my cheeks and I let them. I sit there for a little while and for some reason no one wanders down, so I have all of the Khumbu to myself. I try to clear my mind and allow my thoughts to wander but my mind keeps coming back to the job that still remains, the real reason we're here—that huge mound of rock called Kala Patthar.

I check my watch. We only have a couple hours of daylight, and it's snowing now. I stand up quickly, turning at the same time, and nearly fall over, my body still resistant to the altitude. I lean on a rock for support, and remarkably Meenakshi takes a picture at that exact moment. Figures.

It's time to go. We take one last look around. The woman who broke down earlier is in bad shape, her head lolls back and she holds her arms and shoulders. She is suffering from acute mountain sickness, a serious reaction to the altitude, potentially deadly if her brain swells or fluid drains into her lungs. Her porters and friends are dividing her gear, and her friends speaking to her loudly, trying to keep her conscious. Two porters lift her between them and move at nearly a run, with two more trailing behind. They will take turns walking/carrying her first to Gorak Shep, then further down to Loboche or even perhaps Pheriche, as descending is the only way to help her and it's too late and the weather too bad for a helicopter rescue. We watch them move down the trail and out of sight, the rest of her team trailing silently behind.

The trek back to Gorak Shep is the most difficult either of us has ever experienced. We gain the ridge again, and almost immediately we are both nauseous, to the point where we must stop every five or ten minutes to let our stomachs settle. It's disconcerting after all this to be so inhibited. In the nearly three hours it takes us to get back to Gorak Shep, the weather changes from swirling rain and mist to snow and then to perfectly clear skies.

I'm furious at my body for betraying me this way, and so suddenly. The final 300 yards across the wide, level Gorak Shep plateau are brutal—we both have to stop every three or four steps. Every few feet I walk feels like I have been punched in the stomach. Every few steps I have to breathe deep, inhaling hard to calm my nerves and my body.

We limp back to our lodge like wounded soldiers. I can barely crest the slight rise in the doorway that leads into the common room.

We both fling ourselves down on our bunks, gasping. I sit at the edge of the bunk for a long time, holding my stomach. When I feel like I can move again, I break out a handful of Pepto Bismol tablets and we gulp them down like candy.

It's a hard evening for us. We order momos and grilled cheese but can't finish our meals. The tomato soup is flavorless and we just curl up in a corner away from the other trekkers and wait for nighttime so we can properly go to bed. The memory of that evening will be surprisingly hazy for both of us, lost in a numb fog of altitude sickness and exhaustion. We go to bed early. Since it's a bunk house, we set up the next day's gear carefully so we won't have to bother anyone the next morning.

Our plan is to leave for Kala Patthar at sunrise, so we crawl into our sleeping bags fully clothed for the next morning.

Neither of us says much that night before drifting off, but we're both thinking the same thing. Tomorrow, we will climb our mountain. Tomorrow, the past year of training and sacrifice will be put to the test. Kala Patthar rises up, just outside our window, impassive, waiting for us.

But even after we have come this far, even after the success of this day, we know we don't have much left in us.

I try to calm my breathing so I can sleep, try to unravel the knots that have formed, and now the doubt has crept in as well.

I fall asleep wondering how we can possibly climb Kala Patthar feeling like this.

Chapter 13
~
Kala Patthar

There is no sound. There is no snow. There is no wind. Gorak Shep is deathly still. It is as if a cloak of cold has pressed down upon the Khumbu, muffling the senses.

We have been in cold so furious and angry that we had to stay constantly vigilant against the insatiable wind to keep it from sneaking under a glove or over a face mask, to protect ourselves against near instant frostbite. We've fought our way up Mount Washington and Mount Jefferson in sideways rain that chilled the spine and slid upward under the hood and threatened hypothermia. We've attempted to outrun lightning on slicked summits, with flashes at our backs and sheets of icy water in our faces.

But this cold . . . this is new. It was a cold night. It was a colder morning, preparing for Kala. But stepping outside the relative warmth of the lodge into *this* cold is shocking.

At 5:45 a.m. the sun has to work extra hard to rise above these mountains, though a morning glow makes headlamps unnecessary. But our hands and feet are immediately, unrelentingly cold. It is like dipping your fingertips into a bucket of ice water. It's that sudden.

By the time we move the fifty yards across the dry lake plateau to the base of Kala, I am balling my fingers into fists under my gloves to keep them warm—my Hestra mountaineering 20-below-zero gloves.

We stand at the base of Kala Patthar next to a signed trailhead. The trail appears to shoot straight up the slope of our mountain. We are small and tired and very, very cold. The walk from the lodge to the trailhead has left me breathless. On the plus side, the early bed and light food appear to have settled our stomachs somewhat. After being in Gorak Shep for nearly twenty-four hours, it seems we are acclimating. No headaches either. Good news.

So, at nearly six a.m. on Friday, October 22, nearly one year since we began our journey to this mountain, we take our first steps and begin to climb.

"Here we go," I say. And as my boot settles on the black frozen earth that is Kala Patthar, I am once again reminded of how amazing it is to be here at all.

Kala Patthar means black rock. The mountain itself is not a technical climb. It is not even a rock scramble, for the most part. It has no specific spiritual meaning or history. It needs no permits. At one time this now-dry lake bed held glacier runoff. Its most recent claim to fame was when the Nepali prime minister and his cabinet held a symbolic and much maligned meeting at the base of Kala to draw attention to climate change. The politicians were helicoptered in, and many needed oxygen to function.

No, Kala's meaning is personal to those who attempt to scale it. Kala becomes part of a trekker's character, part of the lives of the thousands who attempt and fail and the thousands who attempt and succeed.

Everest is unattainable to most. Kala is attainable to all but still requires enough discipline and sacrifice to change your life.

We start slow, going at a 25/10 pace—twenty-five steps, ten breaths. This works for a while as we scale the first of three tiers of the mountain. I manage to keep my heart from exploding and the headaches from creeping up my spine. The pace does little to warm our hands and feet, though, and we're constantly flexing our fingers and toes to maintain circulation.

We reach the first tier and take a long break. A small group of trekkers stumble around, trying to keep warm but at the same time trying to drink in the views. Even here, at about 17,300 feet, the views are wonderful. The sun is creeping up from the east and is directly behind Everest, creating a golden halo behind the tip of the peak. The top of Pumori shines blinding white.

Kala Patthar is technically a shoulder of Pumori. Its left and right sides are cliffs, while its summit point also falls off down to the ridge that eventually works its way up to Pumori.

We hike across the flat section of the first tier, circle around a slight bulge in the ridge and the remaining two tiers come into view. From here, we can see the prayer flags at the summit, tiny blue and red pinpricks against the white background of Pumori. It is a mile and 1,000 feet away.

"That's the summit?" Meenakshi asks. "All that way. I don't know if I can do this."

Such hesitation is common here. Many trekkers make it no farther than this first tier. The views of Everest are excellent, and depending on their situation, even guides will sometimes only lead trekkers this far.

That is not going to be us, though. Meenakshi has pushed me through walls of fatigue more times than I can count. Now it's my turn.

"We can do this," I say between wheezes. "We made it this far, we can see it through."

Two things happen then. First, the sun finally makes it out from behind Everest, and it's a game-changer. The effect is like walking from a restaurant freezer to a greenhouse—the change is that quick. I can literally feel my fingers warming and within a few minutes I am able to strip off my gloves and unzip my jacket. Both of us turn our faces to the sun and close our eyes.

Second, we run across a young French trekker off the side of the trail, clearly in trouble. We have seen him off and on for a couple days—back in Tengboche he stayed in our lodge—but we have never communicated. He sits on a rock, turned toward the summit, head in his hands. At first I think he's crying.

"Are you OK?" I ask.

He knows nearly no English and I know nearly no French. But he can see that we're concerned and understands the question enough to do something that I'll never forget.

He shakes his head and squats down as though on a toilet, sticks his tongue out and says, "Psssbbbbbt!" Maybe it's the altitude, but it suddenly seems like the funniest thing I've ever seen and I laugh, and Meena laughs and soon even the diarrhea-plagued Frenchman is laughing. And there we are, the two of us in the shadow of Mt. Everest laughing with this poor man who has come so far and is now suffering so badly. I have no clue whether it will help him or not, but I pop out two Pepto Bismol tablets and fold them into his hand.

I gesture to my mouth. "Eat them, eat."

He looks at the tablets then at me then at the tablets again.

I squat down and repeat his "pssssbbbbt!" then say "Fixes diarrhea, good for stomach." I rub my stomach.

And he shrugs and eats the tablets. Just like that I have had a conversation with a Frenchman about diarrhea!

"You can do this," I say and point up toward the summit. "We'll do this together."

He shakes his head sadly, "No, no."

So we leave him there holding his stomach and continue our climb. Warmed by the sun, we move slightly to the left and begin the long turn toward the summit. It's clearer now, the flags up there snapping in the breeze. An hour has passed since we began and we're holding our own.

The day is flawlessly clear. Wispy clouds shimmer around the high peaks, and a stiff summit wind is creating spindrift off the world's highest mountain, creating a ribbon of snow at 29,000 feet. Everest is mesmerizing, and we spend too much time watching it.

"Hey, look!" Meenakshi suddenly calls out.

It's the Frenchman, and he's on the move. His head is down and his hands are still over his stomach but he's moving up. We wait for him to reach us and he throws himself down on a rock, gasping.

I press my hand into his shoulder. "OK, we're going to do this," I say. He looks up at me and I point at myself, then at Meenakshi, then at the distant summit. "Three of us. Together."

I move my forefinger and middle finger in a walking motion, then point again at the summit. He nods, and the sun roars down heat and my legs feel like melting rubber, and Meenakshi is breathing in tiny gasps and the Frenchman clutches his stomach. But we are a little team now, brought together by the air and the rock. And we *will* reach that summit.

Meenakshi and I fall automatically into caretaker mode. I take the lead, the Frenchman falls in behind to mimic my pace, and Meenakshi picks up sweep.

We reach the second tier in fits and starts, by counting in tens. I take ten steps. They follow. We all take ten breaths. An hour passes this way, three dots praying our way up the mountain, each step becoming a small victory.

We stop before the third tier to hydrate and eat something. It is a place of such extreme raw beauty that it's difficult to put it into the context of anything any of us has ever seen. We stand in a small col between the second and third tiers, a mercifully flat area where we can rest. To our left is a nearly sheer cliff that drops straight down to Pumori's southern valley. To our right, another cliff, this one shooting straight down to Pumori's northern valley. We're only 500 feet away from Kala's summit now, maybe a quarter mile.

"This is it," I say. "Dig deep, we're going to do this."

We begin again, the three of us reaching for anything that's left. Suddenly each step seems more impossible than the last. I find myself taking two, perhaps three steps before bending over and sucking wind. There are boulders here, on the summit cone, more like what we have in the Whites, only 10,000 feet higher. I start searching for paths around rocks, rather than having to step up and over them, which is much harder.

The final thirty minutes of climbing is the hardest I've ever done. By the time we are fifty feet from the summit, my legs are shaking and I can only move one step at a time before taking ten breaths.

"Are you OK?" I ask the Frenchman.

He gives me a thumbs up. I motion for him to move ahead of me. He resists for a moment, but is too tired to protest and moves on toward his summit. Meenakshi catches up to me and moves past, understanding what I am doing.

No one conquers mountains. If you are found to be worthy, the mountains will let you stand on their summit for a few minutes. Over the years, that sort of humility in the face of the wilderness has helped me get back down, not take chances, be a good caretaker.

Now, I practice one final habit developed over the years. I led this team here, and I make one final offering to the mountain by letting my teammates summit first—a silent but important moment for me to ask for a final and safe passage for us all.

I close my eyes, for only a moment, and take a long deep breath. Then I take the final few steps to the top of our mountain. In ten more minutes, I am there, and it is done.

The first person I see is the Frenchman. The strain he feels shows in his face, but he smiles broadly and throws his arms around me, and I shamelessly hug him back, each of us pounding each other on the back and high-fiving like we are childhood friends.

"Congratulations," I say, but my voice is raw and weak under the wind.

Meenakshi is sitting nearby, resting against the aluminum pole that holds a string of prayer flags. She smiles as I approach and I'm overcome with pride and awe at this woman who, incredibly, is my wife.

"We did it," I say.

"It's incredible."

From Kala Patthar, the entire eight miles of the Khumbu Glacier rolls like a tongue down from Mt. Everest. The expanse is so great that we see the glacier as a curve instead of the straight line it is. Everest, Nuptse, Lotse, Pumori, Ama Dablem and dozens of peaks in all directions shimmer against a royal blue sky. Far below, at the base of a glacier lake, we can see a dozen yellow and red tents in Pumori Base Camp. From here, the icefall is a jagged band of white points, spread out along the mouth of the glacier.

It is enormous. It is a view that we worked nearly a year to attain and it is worth it beyond any reasonable explanation.

It is 9:49 a.m. We have nowhere to go, nowhere to be and no desire to leave. If I don't move around too much, I can breathe without having to take giant gulps of air. Incredibly, the temperature hovers in the 20s, and even the wind is not a hindrance.

So we sit at 18,350 feet and soak it all in. The tears were shed yesterday. Today we bathe in the accomplishment, in the magnificent mountain that called us so long ago, in the strength we gained from the effort and in the bright wonderful future that awaits us back home.

There are a lot of people coming and going, and we wait for a lull to scramble up to the steep and pointed actual summit. A giant mound of prayer flags sits in a jumble at the summit, which is only about four feet wide with steep drop-offs on two of its three sides. I pull out my sister's prayer flag one last time and tie it to the jumble of fabric, leaving it in the Khumbu, hoping its positive karma will reach out to all who suffer like she does and, maybe, make them feel better for just a moment.

Meenakshi comes up to the summit with me and a kind man below takes our picture, the only shot of us at the true summit as it turns out, laughing, gasping, gripping the rocks tightly.

We scramble back down, find a tight little corner away from trekkers and take pictures. We drink. We eat some cheese, and we talk aimlessly about the sun, and the silver peaks, and the wedding, and the way our breath feels so high up. And we put our arms around each other, and grin stupidly, and I laugh out loud at nothing and everything.

There are no words. We are wonderfully alive, and together. We are a team, and the universe spreads out before us.

We can do anything.

Chapter 14
~
Pointing Our Boots Toward Home

I throw myself headlong atop my sleeping bag, barely able to squirm out of my boots, to say nothing of actually getting inside the bag. Meena is already asleep in the bunk across the way.

It's early afternoon. The sun still shines. The thrill of the day has not abated. But our original plan—to leave Gorak Shep and overnight at lower altitude in Loboche or Dughla—now seems laughable. What were we thinking?

We took our time climbing down off Kala Patthar, letting adrenaline and gravity do as much work as possible. But it was still work. We paused often, drinking in the spectacular views and enjoying the feeling that comes with being a trekker "heading down." We had graduated. We had degrees in summiting Kala Patthar, and in tagging Base Camp. We now had knowledge. The magic information of the trails ahead, the conditions, the lodging, was at our fingertips.

It felt so good.

But as we huffed down to the second, then first tier, and as we made our way across the long dry plateau between the mountain and the village, there was no question of our moving on today.

We evaluated. No headaches. No dehydration. Slight nausea. Extreme exhaustion.

We made the decision to stay one more night in Gorak Shep, one more night at 17,000 feet, and try to get some rest for the trek back rather than risk total meltdown halfway to Loboche.

That meant two things. First, we hadn't booked anything for that night. But it was only about two p.m., that perfect time between those who had left and those who were yet to come, and we managed to snag a real room. The price was high, about $20, but we did not care. We dragged our gear from the bunkhouse to the room, which seemed gloriously luxurious. We boldly resisted sleeping immediately, and dragged our sorry legs into the dining room and ordered a cup of soup and a grilled cheese sandwich and lemon tea, and we sat in a corner, anti-social, and huddled close together and barely managed to get that food down.

We had earned our solitude. After only about twenty minutes, though, we were done.

I made one more stop. Down a flight of stone stairs, the plywood shack that served as an Internet café was open, so I didn't realize the teenage caretaker was asleep under a filthy blanket by the door.

"I'm so sorry, dhia!" I said, addressing him as an elder even though he was twenty-five years my junior as a way of being apologetic.

But he didn't seem to mind and soon the generator was humming and I wrote this as my update on Facebook:

On Fri. Oct. 22 at 9:49 am Nepal time, M and I summited 18,250 ft Kala Patthar! The climb was cold and hard, but skies perfectly clear and we were able to spend 30 minutes basking in the glow of Everest. Tears were shed. Thank u all for your well wishes. It's hard to describe how bone achingly tired and joyously happy we are at the same time! It's time to come home . . .

I have no energy to write more or try to upload photos, so I join Meenakshi in our room. She is already snoring, just a lump inside her sleeping bag and under a quilt. After the first week or so, we made a contest out of seeing who could get into our room first. The first one there has the honor of taking off their boots, and filling the room with the bathless smell for the second to enjoy. She clearly won this round! But even the nearly overpowering smell of yak dung and sweat do not deter me.

I am asleep in two minutes.

The rest does us good. Later in the evening, as we wait for our dinner and the dining hall fills with a new set of trekkers, we share a table with two young men from the States—one from Boston and the other from Denver. They have been trekking around Nepal and India for weeks on a shoestring budget, sleeping in the cheapest hovels and dives and "eating peanut butter with our fingers," one says.

They have just climbed up and over the Kongma La Pass, a col near Mehra Peak nearly as high as Kala Patthar itself. And now, after tagging Base Camp, they are planning on climbing Kala tomorrow and returning via the Cho La Pass. Ambitious. And crazy considering their worn boots and threadbare gear. Ah, youth! They are scruffy and pleasantly naive, and they chat amicably with us about their exploits and we find like-souls in their enthusiasm and in our mutual disdain for commercial trekking groups.

The boys are far more vocal about it. "What's the point of doing this if you don't do it on your terms?" one says.

We could remind them that a large percentage of the Nepali economy in this region depends upon commercial trekking groups and guide services, but we enjoy their company and energy far too much to argue. Instead we decide to pay forward our good fortune.

Days earlier I bought us two Snickers bars to eat at the summit of Kala Patthar. The bars came up with us, but we were too tired and cold to eat them then. So we present them to the boys, and the four of us unwrap the candy and pass it around—an offering of thanks for our success and hope for theirs.

That amazing day ends on an unforgettable note. There is a general shuffle of people heading back outside into the frigid evening. The moon is rising. We follow a group and make our way down to the center of the dry lake bed fifty yards from the dim lights of Gorak Shep.

We are sore, and tired, and shivering, but as we turn to the east, the magical sight of the moon cresting the tip of Mt. Everest brings a surreal and beautiful end to the day.

In twelve hours, Meenakshi and I have been allowed to watch the sun, then the moon, rise over the highest mountain on Earth. Astonishing.

Chapter 15
~
Three Days Up, Eight Hours Down

The day begins with Hello Kitty.

After a week and a half on the trail, Meena and I have developed a reputation, something that often happens on long journeys like this where word travels by foot and a favorite pastime of residents is trail talk.

We've met enough locals along the way to either earn their grudging respect or simply bewilder them by what they consider an odd sight—an upper-crust Brahmin native Nepali who understands the language and speaks it with a Chicago Rust Belt accent and a no-nonsense attitude is hiking to Everest Base Camp with a skinny shaved-headed white boy who mangles the language every chance he gets, eats whatever is put in front of him and carries a stuffed Hello Kitty.

The Sherpas have shaken their heads as they passed us and laughed. On the way down, Meena overheard one say "look at the little kitten on his pack!" The porters begged and pleaded with us often to let them carry our gear, disbelieving that we'd be able to handle it and telling us terrible stories of tragedies that befell trekkers who tried to do it themselves. And the other trekkers? Well, more than once they seemed startled and confused that my personal guide appeared to be a 12-year-old Nepali girl.

But now we are *heading down*. We have summited Kala Patthar *and* tagged Base Camp. We have mountain cred.

And amazingly, as we crawl out of bed on the tenth day of our trek, we feel good. We are well rested. We eat ravenously at breakfast that morning, bread and cheese and fried eggs. All those trekkers we knew are long gone, having turned back, having tagged and left or having gone off through some other pass. It feels like we are the last to leave the mountain.

I realize this morning, as we step outside into the blazing morning sun and swing our packs onto our shoulders, that we have acclimated! After six days above 14,000 feet, I can breathe and my legs have lost their wobble. We are cold, sure. Tired, you bet. But to be that high and to feel that normal, suddenly, is like getting a shot of adrenaline.

So, to celebrate our success and pay homage to the mountains that will now be at our backs, I pull Hello Kitty out of my pack and strap her to the back of it, a white and red fuzzy mascot for those who follow behind us.

A few years ago, when my niece was three years old, she adored Hello Kitty. She talked to Hello Kitty. She made elaborate, detailed life plans with Hello Kitty. So I began talking back. On our trips, we'd drag this little Hello Kitty stuffed doll with us and take pictures to send to my niece: Hello Kitty in the Grand Canyon, Hello Kitty on Route 66, Hello Kitty in Chicago, and so forth. I'd email her the pictures as Hello Kitty, tell her about my adventures as Hello Kitty, and we became pen pals.

Now, she is older, and the kitty with the red ribbon doesn't seem to hold her interest as much under the glaring sleekness of Barbie. Since I'm damned if I'm going to fasten a Barbie to my pack, Hello Kitty has stayed and become my mascot and personal talisman.

So off we go, back over the narrow spine of the glacier, down into the first valley, past the Italian Research Center and finally back to Loboche, where we once again greedily devour a lunch of soup and grilled cheese and tea. Not wasting any time, we are back on the trail before noon, shooting down the valley, clambering back over the Khumbu Glacier runoff and finally making it in one lightning descent to the somber memorial garden atop the glacier's terminal moraine.

There, we rest, and marvel at our speed! And as we sit on the sun-warmed rocks, sipping water and not saying much, we spy a curious thing. High up on the rocks, overlooking the Pheriche Valley, above the memorial chortens and monuments, is a painter. A large Japanese man sits in a folding chair, facing an easel, painting the amazing Ama Dablem. From that vantage point, the mountain careens up out of the Earth, a towering force of ice and rock. The man's red jacket billows in the wind, but his gaze is soft and focused. He is taking his time, and it is quite beautiful.

After a while we notice that the afternoon clouds have begun to creep into the Pheriche Valley. It's time to go.

We drop down the glacier moraine and it feels like we are flying. With every step my breathing becomes easier, my feet feel lighter. Trekkers huff past us, heads down, sweat pouring from their brows. I wonder if we looked like that a few days ago. Back in Dughla we stop for a quick milk tea and relax along the same stone wall we commandeered last time we were here.

We continue back into the valley and as we walk once again through the yak herder village known as Tsambur, we stumble across an amazing sight, an entire pen of baby yaks. Given that yaks are generally born between May and June, these little guys must be about four months old. They squeal a little bit, sort of like angry guinea pigs, and appear quite shy, not wanting to wander too close to the stone fence as long as we are there.

They aren't exactly cute, more like smaller versions of their moms and dads.

The domestic yaks of Nepal and Tibet are remarkable creatures. The hearts and lungs of the beasts are larger than those of the cattle found at lower altitudes, so they are well adapted to the high plateaus. In fact, so adapted are they that yaks at lower altitudes with temperatures over sixty degrees will begin to suffer from heat exhaustion because they have nearly no sweat glands.

So ingrained in the Tibetan culture are these 2,000-pound steamrollers that sports have begun to crop up around them: yak racing and yak polo are common now and being marketed as tourist attractions in some central Asian countries.

Our babies are a ways away from the polo grounds, and aside from keeping their distance have no interest in us whatsoever, so we move on to Pheriche, arriving as a cold wind and light mist begin to cover the town.

It has taken us eight hours to descend what took us three days to climb.

We receive one more pleasant surprise that day. We make a bee-line to the Nagarkot, of course, hoping that little Chori Tenzing and her mom might have a room for us. Upon entering the familiar lodge, we are greeted with a profound welcome.

"You made it!" the lodge mistress says. "We were worried!"

It turns out that once again Lene Oh has inserted himself into our hike. After running across us three days ago, that crazy little man did some calculations in his head and figured we'd be back down to the Nagarkot yesterday evening. He had reserved rooms for us! When we didn't arrive yesterday, the lodge owners became worried. Plus, there were no rooms available at the lodge today.

But incredibly, thinking that perhaps we'd arrive tonight, she walked into town where her sister runs the Shangri-la Lodge, and reserved rooms there for us. Try finding service like that at the Hilton.

We are enormously grateful and more than a little shocked at the trouble they went through for us. It's easy for a jaded Westerner to look at such tactics as simple consumer capitalism, but it really went above and beyond. We immediately and graciously accept the room at the Shangri-la.

And as it turns out, that evening's dinner and conversation are some of the funniest of the trip. Now that we are on our way down, we figure anything goes, so we order our first meat dish in over a week. We decide to try yak meat. Spicy.

A few words about eating yak, things we can appreciate only in retrospect. Yaks are the lifeblood of the Khumbu. Supplies are carried on their backs. Yak dung is the only source of heat. Yaks are used to plow the fields. Yak wool is used to make clothes to keep people warm. Without yaks, survival in these parts would be considerably more difficult. They are the Khumbu equivalent of purebred race horses. A family's pride, reputation, success and perhaps survival depend on yaks.

That being the case, why in heaven's name would a local want to use a yak as food—particularly as food for trekkers? The answer is, they would not.

So the plate of sizzling yak meat placed on our table was likely from a yak that was no longer a breadwinner. Perhaps the yak was too old to do any more heavy lifting. Maybe the poor guy tripped and went into a gorge and they fished him out to serve. Maybe he had a disease, or a condition that made him less able to be of practical use.

Whatever the case, our yak is just terrible. The dish smells delicious, but the meat is tough and gamy and leaves an awful aftertaste. We can't eat it.

With us this evening is a group of eight young trekkers from the Czech Republic. Only a couple speak English, but we enjoy spending the evening with them primarily because they pump us for as much information as they can get. We are "going down." They are "going up," you see.

After nibbling around the edges of our yak dish, we offer the whole thing to them. They are tired, hungry and young, but even they cannot stomach the yak meat. They pass the dish around, and Meena and I laugh at their reactions.

Later, our lodge owner's brother, a teenager home from Kathmandu for the holiday, asks if he can put on some music. Eager to please his young Western guests, the young man has a CD of Western pop. Imagine our surprise when the sweet, mellow sounds of Rick Astley pour out from that beat-up little CD player. Rick-rolled at 14,000 feet! The room exploded in laughter.

After listening for a while, I ask the young man if he has any traditional Nepali music he can play. The poor fellow's face just drops. Apparently he had thought we were cool.

The evening ends this way, listening to Nepali folk music, entertaining the Czech kids with our tales of Base Camp and feeling strong and accomplished. Sleep is easy tonight, and there is no chill in the air.

Chapter 16
~
The Dancing Monks of Mani Rimdu

The young monk arches his back, sucks in as much air as he can, leans over the enormous ceremonial bugle, and blows.

"Brauwwwwwwwk!" Again. "Brauwwwwwwwk!"

Over and over, he and his companion blow into their instruments. There is no difference in tone. The six-foot bugle can play only one note, and in the square courtyard of Tengboche Monastery, that one note echoes off the surrounding mountains like an air siren.

The single-note song accompanies eight dancing monks, dressed as colorful, tantric magicians. They do a slow-motion turn on the heels of their pointy shoes.

"Brauwwwwwwwk!"

This is the amazing and perplexing annual Mani Rimdu Festival, the sacred Buddhist Dance Drama enacted by the monks of Tengboche, and we have front-row seats.

We sit on the steps of the courtyard entrance, about five feet above the courtyard stage, right next to the bugle monks. During an unaccompanied moment, the teenage monk sheepishly reaches into his robes and removes a small digital camera. He snaps a couple quick pictures of his fellow, older, monk dancers, and just makes it back to his bugle in time for another low, deep "Brauwwwwwwwk!"

I'm delighted to watch this unfold. I wonder who he'll send the photos to; his family, I suppose, in some other small village someplace in the Khumbu. He is a monk, but he's a student also, and like all students, over every subject, everywhere, he doesn't take things too seriously.

The midday sun shines gloriously down on the courtyard as we watch the dances unfold.

After a bittersweet goodbye this morning to Chori Tenzing and her mother, we left Pheriche under a deep azure sky, and beelined for Tengboche. We knew that the festival was sometime around when we would be near, but only last night were we told that the Dance, the main attraction and high day, would be taking place on the exact day that we would be trekking through. We were determined to haul all the way back to Namche Bazaar, and along the way, we'd stop in Tengboche to witness the largest and most important Buddhist festival in the Khumbu.

We got an early start and climbed out of the Pheriche Valley, back over the plateau where we celebrated Deshain a week earlier, back down through the mani gate, and past the numerous small villages. On our trip up, we were lost in a fog of rain and freezing wind. But today, the valley weather is perfect and beautiful. Ama Dablem from this perspective is startling, a massive double hump of white, visible from everywhere. We stopped often to take pictures.

As we approached Tengboche, the local crowd became thicker; Sherpa families hurried along the trail toward the festival, which attracts tourists and locals from all through the region. At one point, a lone, skinny Sherpa girl, perhaps eight years old, flew by us, beckoning us to walk with her to Tengboche. But alas, even acclimatized and even going down we were no match for her and she moved breezily through the valley in a T-shirt, shorts and flip-flops.

Admittance to the dance was steep for Westerners, 500 rupees, but we eagerly paid the monk at the outside door and stepped into a completely different world. Tim and Karen had already been there for three days waiting for the dance. We could not imagine staying in Tengboche that long. Karen had started feeling ill.

Like most traditions and festivals in Nepal, the meaning of the rites depends entirely on who you ask and who is writing about it. For example, the Mani Rimdu Festival takes place over either a couple days or two weeks. It involves either about a dozen or fifty monks and Buddhist officials. There are three or four dances or there are a dozen dances. The festival is a ritualistic passion dance that serves to introduce the lay community to the history and concepts of Buddhism, or it is simply a socially enjoyable gathering, much like a Western carnival. Ask one of the monks which of those things Mani Rimdu is, and he will likely just smile and say "Yes."

We have learned by now to let these sorts of experiences wash over us like a cool wind.

Prior to our arrival, a ceremonial yak was anointed in butter in a symbolic offering to Everest, or Miyolangsangma. The lucky yak was then released to wander freely in the valley.

The dances themselves incorporate symbols of demons, such as anger, greed and jealousy, that are obstacles to Buddhist faith. The monks must battle with the dancers dressed as demons.

And it's not just for show, either. Most of the tourists understand the festival in terms of theater, but for many locals, the lamas at Tengboche are the heroes of the Everest region. A local family from a small village in the Khumbu going to the Tengboche Mani Rimdu Festival to watch the lamas face off and conquer the obstacles of Buddhist faith is the equivalent of a family from the Great North Woods going to Fenway to watch the Red Sox beat the Yankees. The only difference might be that the Red Sox fans hate the Yankees more than the Sherpas hate the demons, but you get the picture.

In one dance the fearsome deities are paraded before the public and then the monks arrive. Using elaborate hand gestures and wielding ceremonial weapons, they tame the demons, an illustration of Tengboche's protective role in the Khumbu. And all through the dances, the horn blows and the bells jangle, and we sit and soak in the good cheer and fine atmosphere of this place, which just one week earlier stretched thin our patience and temper.

We spend over an hour in Tengboche, far too much time considering the long walk still ahead of us, but we feel strong and the weather holds and we don't want to cut short our experience of the dances.

We tackle the long climb down, then up with vigor this time, and the afternoon goes by quickly and easily. The lower we trek, the stronger we feel. And thoughts of Namche and the Yak Hotel and electricity and a good plate of momos keep us moving at a breakneck pace.

In fact, our spirits are so high, one important caution slips our mind. As the day creeps by and dusk begins to fall, we realize we are still three miles from Namche on the long valley-hugging path that leads around the cliffs to the town. Earlier in the week, we heard stories about trekkers being mugged after dark in just this area, and it's nearly at this moment that I spot a lone figure standing at a turn in the valley, nearly dead center of the trail.

But as we approach, we realize it's a sleepy porter. He has made not one but two treks back and forth to Ama Dablem Base Camp that day, nearly twice the miles in one day that we trekked, with two full loads on his back. And now, he waits for us in the hope that we can accompany him back to Namche. We have never encountered a tired porter, and we gladly offer him company and conversation. Well, I offer the company while Meenakshi offers the conversation.

The sun has set and we're beat by the time we drag up to The Yak Hotel. The fine proprietor, Chime Kalden Sherpa, who had been so kind to us a week earlier, never misses a beat. He welcomes us home and personally escorts us not to a regular room but to the hotel's guest room. So eager is he to have us stay that, since all the regular rooms are occupied, he lets us stay in his personal space. The room is warm, and not plywood, and the mattress is as soft as a feather. Once again, we're humbled by the service of our hosts. Not only do we eagerly accept his room, but we decide to treat ourselves to a hot shower as well!

There is no soap, and no shampoo and the concrete floor could use a good scrub down. But I have forgotten what hot water feels like on my skin, and as the dirt and sweat slip free from my body, an enormous wave of exhaustion overtakes me, and I let it.

Dinner this evening, in the warm, clean common room, is rice and chili and momos, and as I sit here in my clean skin, contemplating how far we have come, and I listen to the anxious conversation of upward-bound trekkers at the table next door, I begin to drift off. We have done it, we have returned to 10,000 feet with no ill effects, no injuries and many, many stories. Tomorrow, we'll rest. We'll sleep in, and shop, and explore Namche.

And maybe we'll even find a good cup of coffee.

Chapter 17

—

Tourists in Namche

When the young Sherpa woman shopkeeper starts throwing punches, we all freeze in place.

Perhaps it's the shock of seeing an actual, down and dirty, fists-flying fight in the middle of the Namche market. Or perhaps it's that nobody really seems to take it seriously. Maybe it's the armed Nepali military guy standing off to the side, smoking, watching.

After all the kindness, goodwill and seemingly peaceful nature of the Khumbu we have experienced up until this point, witnessing a fight in broad daylight in the middle of one of the most heavily tourist-populated streets in town is amazing. Nobody does anything. We don't do anything.

But then, when the older Sherpa woman, who so far has been on the receiving end of most of the punches, picks up a large, heavy walking stick, the honorary mayor of Namche finally steps in.

Yak Hotel owner Chime Kalden has had enough. He gets between the women and I don't need to understand the language to know what he says. This is bad for business. Tourists are watching. Take it inside. The two women stalk off, grumbling, cursing each other over their shoulders. And slowly life returns to normal.

"Crazy, huh?" a voice says beside me. It's Tim! He and Karen finally made it out of Tengboche and as coincidence has it are also staying at the Yak Hotel, but Karen is sick and Tim has run down to find some stomach meds. If I had stayed for four days in Tengboche, I would have been ill as well.

We feel bad for Karen, but it's late in the day and we're happy to see a friendly face.

This morning we slept in, not leaving the comfort of the Yak Hotel until nine a.m. We were beat, but elated. We ate ravenously at breakfast, brushed our teeth, ran cold, cold water over our heads and washed our faces. I used a Western toilet. It was heaven. We luxuriated in a world that had suddenly and wonderfully become slow and perfect. The weather was warm, and we strolled through the streets and trails of Namche without a care in the world and no deadline or elevation to tackle.

After breakfast, we wandered up a long, nearly hidden trail to a deep overhang and rock wall that we found out are used in the annual Dumjee Festival, a boisterous affair that celebrates the accomplishments of a local lama. Participants dress in their finest wear and Sherpa elders toss handfuls of tsampa—barley flour—at the rock outcropping, which they believe watches over the town.

We followed the trail to the farthest northern corner of the town, where it breaks out over the ridge, and discovered a helicopter pad settled into the very edge of the cliff, thousands of feet above the Milk River. We watched in amazement as a yak herder brought the shaggy beasts down to the platform to take inventory before heading into town.

On the way back to town, we wandered over to Namche Monastery, a beautiful, deeply colorful building far older than its more popular sister in Tengboche. Inside, a lone monk swept the floor of the prayer room as Meena and I sat before the detailed murals and soaked in the warmth and smells of the ancient building. Meena helpfully translated the monk's words for trekkers as they came in, and for a little while we became docents to other trekkers' journeys.

We visited the Sherpa Life Museum, a wondrous place created by a deaf Sherpa named Lhakpa Sonam, who survived a 200-foot avalanche on a Swiss expedition and traveled all over Europe and America for his education. Here, he ran a museum, a library and a lodge and curated the largest collection of Sherpa climbing artifacts likely in the world.

For lunch, we decided to go Western. It was a terrible mistake. A small outdoor café near the center of town provided us with a rich menu of Western lunch options. I ordered a personal pizza while Meena picked a cheese sub. The pizza was a soggy mess of uncooked dough under a gooey smear of burned yak cheese. Meena's sandwich was even worse, so bad, in fact, that we took a picture. The Khumbu version of a cheese sub apparently was grated cold yak cheese and sliced tomatoes atop a thick bed of yellowing salty mayonnaise. Neither of us could eat the thing. We laughed, understanding what Nepalis apparently thought our Western food was like.

And now, as dusk begins to settle over Namche and our sense of calm satisfaction over our trip buzzes pleasantly in our heads, we do the only thing left to do: We shop.

We each buy a new pair of hiking socks and liners to make our final long push back to Lukla tomorrow more comfortable. We buy new wicking shirts and immediately change into them.

Finally, Meena leaves me in the Internet café as she goes to barter with a shop owner over a spectacular Marmot jacket I've had my eye on. It is a fake, of course, as most high-end gear here is, but it looks so . . . European! I have to have it. And by this time we know that if a white boy shows up the price will be twice as high. Sure enough, a grinning Meena appears twenty minutes later having bought the jacket for 1,700 rupees, about $35. The deal of the trip.

Later, as we sit in the common room, eating dinner, our host tells us the story of the fighting Sherpa women, both shopkeepers. The older woman had accused the younger one's son of stealing from her shop. It was a slight that normally would be dealt with out of public, after hours. But the older woman had no credibility with other Namche shopkeepers. She recently opened her store and dared to compete with other business owners, breaking the unwritten Namche rule of solidarity and equal pricing.

Capitalism had split Namche and erupted into a street fight. I don't know whether to laugh or cry.

We stay up later than normal this evening, taking a walk through the streets after dark, wandering no place in particular, wearing our new clothes like tourists, feeling warm and content.

In a side alley, away from anyone who could see, I give Meena a squeeze and kiss the top of her head, wanting my joy at being here to include her presence as well. Tomorrow we'll aim for Lukla. If all goes well, in two days we'll be on a plane heading for New York.

The trek is winding down, and even as I stand on its narrow streets, I already miss Namche Bazaar.

Chapter 18
〜
Return to Lukla

Karen is still sick. She slept nearly all of the day and evening yesterday, and though feeling better this morning, is nowhere near being well. Perhaps it's the altitude. Maybe she ate something that did not sit well.

Whatever the case, as we get ready to leave Namche, Tim has packed most of her gear in his pack, and we offer to stick with them on the way back.

The difference between Namche and Lukla is only about 1,000 feet of altitude, but it's ten miles. There are a lot of ups and downs and even though we are ready to hit the road at seven a.m., the day is already hot and the sky cloudless.

After breakfast, as we make the final checks of our gear, our host offers one final gesture that nearly brings tears to our eyes. He gives each of us a kati scarf, a lightweight, gold offering of safe travel. We each bow forward as he wraps them around our necks.

I truly feel like a traveler, and I know now I'll miss this place more than any other.

On the way out of Namche, we see an emergency helicopter leaving the pad we explored yesterday and I wonder who's aboard.

Our final day of walking begins serenely enough. We are acclimatized now. Our bellies are full and we've had two full evenings of sleep. We keep track of Karen, who is clearly tired, and try to cheer them both with stories and conversation. Tim is concerned, though, and sometimes seems obsessed with getting her down to some relative safety. He'll move ahead, then seem frustrated when we're unable to follow at that speed. Even healthy, we're no match for Tim's speed and strength. We move like this, a little mismatched foursome, back down the Namche plateau and past beautiful look-outs that were covered in mist on our way up.

At one such switchback in the path, there is a kind, older woman selling small wrinkled oranges she has lined up on a blanket alongside the path. Buying one is tempting, but we pass.

We cross back over the high suspension bridge, then move down to the shores of the Milk River once again. At this stage Karen's spirits seem to lift and we bid our friends farewell. We'll see them again at some point in Lukla, but for now they appear driven enough to move much faster than us.

Here in the sun, at the edge of the river, the valley is magical. I spend some time taking pictures of the white, foamy water. It's roaring so loudly we have to move close to each other to hear. We move at a pleasant pace, past vast cabbage orchards and back through the villages we struggled through a week and a half ago.

We come again to Dingboche and stop for an early lunch amid the marigolds. There we meet a team of three climbers, two Westerners and one Sherpa, who have just finished their expedition to Mera Peak. Even though they have scaled a vastly more difficult and technical peak than us, they are gracious and curious and we share our stories of our successes with each other. Once again, Meena and I are amazed at the obvious differences between the Sherpa guides and the Sherpa climbers. This Sherpa is lean, and broad-shouldered, wearing expensive sunglasses and fine outerwear. No flip-flops here.

A half hour later, we're back in Ghat, the site of our original night. We have an important task to attend to here. Days earlier, a Sherpa guide Meena chatted with asked her to inform his wife that he would be several days late in getting home. He was going to accompany a client the long way back, over the Cho La Pass. Could we tell his wife as we passed through?

I marvel over this simple but crucial responsibility as we search for the man's house. There are no addresses, of course. Meena has a vague description of the house and the Sherpa's name. No email. No phone. No post office. This is how messages are sent from village to village.

After a few inquiries we find the lodge, and find the woman, a child on her waist. She and Meena chat for a while, and we're done. She invites us to stay, but we politely decline, wanting to reach Lukla by that evening.

Afternoon comes quickly. About two miles from Lukla we're startled to run into Tim, who is heading in the other direction. It turns out Karen was too tired to make it all the way to Lukla, so they got a room in Dingboche. Then Tim went on to Lukla to confirm their flight for the next day and is now coming back. I am impressed by his strength but horrified to hear that the Tara Airlines office in Lukla closes at four p.m. and we must confirm today in order to assure our flight for tomorrow.

A word again about domestic travel in Nepal. We have our tickets. The tickets are paid for. We are scheduled to leave Lukla and fly to Kathmandu tomorrow.

In Nepal, that means nothing.

It's 2:30 p.m. and we're two miles from Lukla. I leave some gear and all my water but a half bottle with Meena. We agree to meet at the Tara Airlines building. I give her a kiss and head out, not exactly at a run, but as near as I can manage.

I make good time too, skirting the valley, and assaulting the final climb up to Lukla within an hour. Even after a traffic jam within a half mile of town thanks to a slow-moving yak train, I manage to scramble into the noise and ruckus of Lukla with ten minutes to spare! A few more blocks and there's the airline building.

And another line.

I groan. Again, in Nepal the word "line" is fairly relative. The line in front of the tiny Tara Airlines building is really more of a rowdy half circle of angry people all talking at the same time. Inside the one-room barn-like building, frazzled airline workers lazily mark down notes on paper grids. No computers. No electricity. Nothing.

Four p.m. comes and goes, and my patience with this system begins to erode. Finally, at 4:30, after I have stood there for nearly forty-five minutes, Meena joins me, a big grin on her face. She knows how things work around here.

I have had enough, and for five minutes all semblance of

wakefulness evaporates and I decide that being nice does not work here. I leave my pack with Meena and begin to cut. I am unapologetic in my rudeness.

A few people eye me, but no one seems surprised. I shove my way to the front of the line and thrust my boarding passes down toward the oldest man at the table, the one who appears to be in charge.

"Dia!" I bark.

He looks up and I shove the tickets into his hand for verification. He takes them, and I see him write our ticket numbers down in the chart that says ten a.m. He scribbles something on the ticket and hands it back to me without looking. We're done. I'm exhausted.

We drag ourselves back to the outskirts of town, as neither of us has any interest in having to deal with the chaos. If anything, Lukla is more riled up than the first time we passed through, and it seems like there are more people; near the center of town, the thump from a second-floor dance club reverberates into the ground. We settle on a small lodge next to the memorial archway and order dinner for later.

After dumping our packs and putting on some warmer clothes, we walk back into town. We have one final thing to do before our trek comes to an end: visit Starbucks.

I order a chai and Meena orders hot chocolate and we both settle back in this familiar setting to relax and calm our jangled nerves. Oddly, the interior of the place looks like a Hawaiian tiki lounge, with wicker chairs and tables and a small bar pushed up against a wall. In an outer room, there is a small Internet café and we're able finally to post some pictures and notes letting people know we'll be back in Kathmandu tomorrow morning.

But of course, we won't. As we sit in the fake Starbucks waiting for our trek to be over, we don't realize just how much more there is to come.

Chapter 19
~
Zen and the Art of Waiting

Wednesday, October 27

On our final day in the Kumbu, it does not take long to lose all the trappings of Buddhist tranquility, and speedily resort to impatient frustration.

We are taught one final lesson this morning as we sit in the tiny Lukla Airport waiting room wondering what to do next. The lesson is the same one we learned, and perhaps forgot, two weeks ago in Kathmandu. That lesson is that in Nepal, more often than not, courtesy and staying inside the lines does not assure you of anything.

We have our tickets back to Kathmandu in hand. They are confirmed for a ten a.m. flight. They are paid for. We are holding them. Flights are coming and going.

That means nothing.

By noon, it becomes clear that leaving this place won't be easy. The dank, tiny terminal at the airport begins to get to me, so I leave Meena and amble toward the end of the runway to clear my head and get some fresh air.

A series of typical delays has once again derailed our ability to get on a plane and get back to Kathmandu. Our situation is fast approaching desperate. Because of the four-day delay when we left for Lukla, coupled with the extra rest day we took in Namche, we now have only twenty-four hours to get back to Kathmandu. Our flight for Hong Kong leaves tomorrow evening. Bad weather is predicted for Lukla tomorrow morning. If we can't get out of here today, it may be quite some time and expense before we are on our way back to the States.

What's creating this situation? Well, weather, for one thing. Even though up here the sky is calm, we're told that windy weather in

Kathmandu has delayed some flights. And in Lukla, one or two late planes can back things up sometimes for days. This in and of itself would not be infuriating. What really would make Buddha blow his top is that we have no way to bribe anybody to get us on a plane.

Commercial trekking groups do. When things get jammed up in Nepal, the people with the most cash move to the front of the line.

We watched all morning as commercial managers boldly walked past us lowly individuals and easily got their groups onto the few planes coming in. There is no first come, first served here. There is only money.

In fact, it got so bad at one point that Meena simply lost it and began attempting to direct the traffic coming into the terminal. A Nepali tour operator would walk in and ignore the crowd of people already there, and Meena would shout, "The line starts back there!" At one point, we physically dragged a trekking group's duffles away from the counter and put them behind us.

It was a fun project and kept us from getting bored, but it did no good. They would just sneer at us or, worse, ignore us completely like a herd of grumbling yaks.

So we waited and we hoped that the monied groups would all take off before the planes stopped coming.

Now as I pick my way through thin alleys and broken stone streets, the fresh air begins to calm my worries a bit, and I'm able to enjoy and appreciate the oddness of Lukla. The only thing that separates me from the short runway is a small chain link fence; in some places, buildings butt nearly right up against the fence.

I am able to walk all the way to the end of the runway, at the edge of the cliff that shoots straight out and down into the valley below. From here I can turn and look back on Lukla. The town is neither beautiful nor particularly functional. There are no planes coming or going now. There's very little foot traffic. The air is calm, and from here I can feel that slight echo of a deep valley surrounded by high mountains.

I close my eyes and listen to the distant wind and try to refocus.

There's only one thing to do. Eat.

Right across from the terminal entrance is a bakery, designed, I think, to look French with what appears to be some Nepalese equivalent of baguettes. I order a chocolate-filled roll, which turns out to be memorable after all.

"Hey, man! What's up?" says a voice from behind me. The two boys from Gorek Shep, the bootless trekkers with whom we shared our Snickers bar, are casually lounging in a corner. Incredibly, they tagged Kala Patthar, detoured around the high Cho La Pass, *and* made it back to Lukla on the same day as us. I am amazed at their endurance, but also a little terrified that there are more potential plane passengers to deal with.

"You guys heading back today?" I ask.

They laugh. "Who knows?" one says. "We don't even have tickets. We just figured we'd play it by ear and see what happens. We'll get back eventually."

And just like that, the tension of this day drains from my shoulders. They sit back in the cafe's fake cast-iron chairs and eagerly slurp the fake, diluted coffee, and the grins on their dirty, unshaven faces tell the story of their adventure. And of mine as well.

I reach out to shake hands. "It's been a real pleasure, guys. You take care of yourselves."

But a handshake isn't enough, and they both jump up to give me a quick hug, loudly slapping me on the back with shouts of "Take care!" and "Great to meet you."

I make my way back to the dusty terminal to find Meena sprawled out across two red plastic seats. I hand her what's left of my chocolate roll and sink pleasantly into the seat next to her.

"You OK?" she asks.

I grin widely. "Never better!" And that's the truth.

The afternoon slips by. There aren't many planes coming or going, and we attempt to get onto each one that does. We make a game of trying to understand the system, something about each airline rotating its flights so that one to four of each airline's planes shows up every hour. But we're not certain. And after a while, we cease to care. If we can get on a plane, fine. If not, we'll march back to a tea house, have momos and try again tomorrow. If we miss our flight to Hong Kong, maybe we'll just hike the extra five days down to Jiro and take a bus back to Kathmandu. There are worse things than being stuck here.

Slowly, as the day wears on, we're joined in the terminal by many of the solo trekkers we ran into on the trail. Tim and Karen are there, with Karen looking pale but certainly better than she did a few days ago. Two Germans whom we recognize as the retching couple from Tengboche march in. And then I'm thrilled when I recognize the Frenchman who became part of our team on Kala Patthar.

I shake his hand, and he rubs his belly and gives me a thumbs up.

And so, here we are, seven wanderers at the end of our journeys. We are absolutely filthy and our clothes hang off us like rags. Most of us don't know each other's language so there's not much talking, but as we gather on a long bench and have someone take our picture together, we are all aware of the bond, forged by miles and mountains, that we share.

We all split whatever food we have left in our backpacks, and I run off to the airport's only, tiny, concession stand and buy some absolutely awful instant coffee.

We do eventually find a plane, one of the last ones coming in from Kathmandu that day. This time, we are able to sit next to each other, and I reach out to hold Meena's hand as the pilot jams the plane full throttle down the tiny runway, dust and dirt kicking up behind us. And at the moment the runway ends and the plane lifts off into the mountain sky, we share a glorious, terrified look and laugh as the pilot strains to see through the foggy windshield. Soon the mountains are just white streaks over our shoulders.

I sink back into the uncomfortable seat and scratch my scrubby chin and it feels like I could sleep for days. Meena leans her head on my shoulder and neither of us talks much for the flight home, lost in the haze of momos and mountains. I remind myself that this woman is also now my wife.

And then, one more small but amazing moment at the very end of our journey. After we debark onto the runway bus in Kathmandu, our driver swings the tiny shuttle around a corner near our terminal. Someone behind me shouts, "Look, look, is that Messner?"

There on the tarmac is the greatest mountain climber in history. In his mid-sixties now, Reinhold Messner could pass for 40. He's unmistakable with his giant shock of gray and black hair and full-on Mountain Man beard. He's lost in the task of giving directions to a group of porters. This is like seeing a rock star, and for a few seconds as we pass, everyone on the bus becomes quiet.

Before Messner, it was thought that climbing Everest without supplemental oxygen was impossible. Then, in 1978, he did it. Solo. Before Messner, no one thought to attempt to climb all fourteen of the 8,000-meter mountains in the world. He finished that list in 1986. He climbed them all without supplemental oxygen. He once described the experience of climbing without O_2 as like "a single, narrow, gasping lung, floating over the mists and summits."

Oh, and he also claims to have seen Yeti.

We all see him for a moment, and the moment is gone. A gift, perhaps, from the Gods; a capstone to our journey?

The shuttle parks near the terminal and we shuffle out. There are no cheering crowds to meet us, no fans to ask for autographs, to marvel at our journey. We are common again as we slowly make our way to the street and sink into a taxi for the ride back to Meena's aunt's house. The chaos of Kathmandu's streets is particularly fierce this late afternoon, but I don't care anymore.

This place feels comfortable to me now, even after the open spaces and clean air of the mountains. Kathmandu feels like a place I could come home to. Any adrenaline we may still have in our bones from the journey long since dissipated in Lukla. Now, we just long for a shower, and perhaps some chicken curry, and maybe a cup of tea at a kitchen table where I can look across at Meena and share a smile only we two will ever understand.

Epilogue
Alone in the Moment

For the first time since I set foot in this unworldly place, I am alone.

Meenakshi and her aunt have set off to spend the afternoon shopping. Her uncle is at work. And all the guests and family who came to our wedding weeks ago are gone.

Our flight leaves in the evening, and I want to make one last circuit of this place, one final lap, even though I don't know if I'll know where I'm going or what I'm doing.

Before leaving, my instructions are that if I get lost I am to just ask a cabbie to take me to the new Chinese embassy. Meena's aunt and uncle live just up the street, and surely I could find my way from there.

I don't think much of it as I set off, a few remaining rupees in my pocket along with a paper bag of peanuts. I'm not going to take a cab. Or a tuk-tuk. Or a rickshaw. I walked to Everest, and I'll walk in Kathmandu as well.

The night before, upon our arrival home, I was able to stand for ten minutes in a hot shower and revel in the simplicity of an act the West takes for granted. Then, before Meenakshi came down to join me, her aunt fed me what to this day is the best meal I have ever had. Rice and goat and chicken. Alu and peppers. Soup and bread and a tall glass of mango lassi. It was magic. It was kingly. I felt like crying from gratefulness.

So now, with a full belly and a deep night's sleep, I begin to walk among the madness, trying to breathe it all in, to be in the moment and explore as I like.

I head south, passing what I think are familiar landmarks: a deep well-like structure at the bottom of which is a curious and ancient-looking altar; the modern and cold Chinese embassy, in whose front courtyard Meena rode her bike as a child, and a tiny shop, stacked from floor to ceiling with cases of something called Playboy whiskey.

After a while, I come to an apartment building I remember as one of Meena's uncle's own and I'm able to recalibrate my location. On a whim, I move off the busy street and stroll into a lonely alley where a small calf is resting in a dank corner.

"Hi, buddy," I say, petting his head. He lifts his big, black eyes and grunts before going back to his nap. At that moment, a pack of Nepali schoolgirls drifts by, a wave of shiny shoes, plaid skirts and gray suit jackets. The uniforms are similar to the ones Meena wore as a schoolgirl. There must be a private Catholic school nearby.

"Namaste, girls," I say. I correct myself and say, "I mean, Bhainis," using what may or may not be the plural form of saluting young women. They collectively burst out laughing, and I know I've mangled the language horribly. But I've given them something to talk about and they are preteens after all so I don't mind.

In the distance I see a large modern structure rising up from above the residential buildings and am surprised to discover a very new mall, full of shiny glass and bustling with the energy of crowds moving up and down the five-story escalator. I blend in with the crowd and make my way up to the fifth floor. There, near the plastic shopping carts and all the trappings of a modern plaza, I look out through the tinted glass over the rooftops and can see the white ridges of the distant Himalayas. It seems impossible to me to be able to see the mountains from here when behind me families with shopping bags and bored smoking men waiting for their wives mull about unimpressed with the view. I wonder whether, if I lived here, I would eventually stop looking as well.

I'm slightly rattled by the experience and head off at a quick clip, suddenly thirsty and looking for a place to rest. In a courtyard, I see the brightly colored umbrella top of a street-side vendor, but

I stop in my tracks after going down a flight of stairs to get a drink from him.

I am at the Snake Pond. This ancient, rectangular courtyard sits in a heavily trafficked area of the city, but it seems to exist in another time. The pond is about the size of a gym swimming pool, but the water is deep green and black and still. Moss clings to the corners and the waterline like a fuzzy curtain.

And there in the center of the pond, rising menacingly out of the water, is King of Naga, the serpent god. This is Nag Pokhari, and I learn later that the serpent is worshiped in a great festival, Nagpanchami Day. A priest will come and make offerings to Naga and patrons will keep pictures of the snake god outside their homes.

According to legend, a prince was once passing by and saw a beautiful girl bathing in the pond. He, of course, instantly fell in love and proposed. She agreed, but only on the condition that once a year she would leave him for twenty-four hours and the prince must never ask or try to discover why she left. Despite their happy marriage, after several years the prince was overcome by curiosity and followed the princess during one of her disappearances.

Not surprisingly, she came to the pond, walked straight into it, and her form changed into a snake. She was the daughter of Naga, or Naga Kanya, a snake girl. When she had fallen in love with a human, her father cursed her into having to return to snake form every year.

And now that her prince had witnessed her transformation, Naga killed the prince. Heartbroken, the princess took her own life. It was Romeo and Juliet, Nepal Style. Now, the two of them are often said to be seen together at Nag Pokhari, sometimes in the gossamer form of a prince and princess and other times as two snakes coiled together in the dark water.

If there is any place in my travels where I would most believe in ghosts, it would be at this ghastly, beautiful place.

The sun is getting low and my time here is drawing to a close. And remarkably, I know where I am and how to get back. To celebrate, I step up to the soda stand and ask for an orange Fanta. The crude sign says "25" and for a moment I am lost in the Kumbu and give the young man 250 rupees, my head not doing the needed calculation that here, in the valley, a Fanta really is only 25 rupees, or about a dime.

It would have been very easy for the proprietor to make a great deal of money that day, to simply take this Westerner's cash and pocket the rest.

But he doesn't.

"Sir, sir," he shouts waving my cash as I'm walking away. "Only 25, only 25!"

He is a good man, and these are a good people. I sit on a low stone wall beside an ancient pond dedicated to a snake god and sip the sweet drink out of a cold glass bottle as the sun sets in Kathmandu. All around me, the million sounds of horns and bikes, and hens and bells, seem to blend into one continuous song. And the afternoon glow on the dust and clouds and pollution creates a rainbow over that green water and I close my eyes and breathe, and the past and future slip off my shoulders until only now remains.

Further Reading

Sir Edmund Hillary, *View from the Summit*, 2000. From the pen of the
   man himself, this is Hillary's own account of his momentous 1953
   ascent of Everest.

Wolfgang Korn, *The Traditional Architecture of the Kathmandu Valley*,
   1998. A fine overview of the traditional architectural style of the
   Kathmandu Valley.

Jon Krakauer, *Into Thin Air*, 1997. In one of the greatest adventure
   books of all time, Krakauer redefined the meaning of adventuring in
   Nepal with his account of the 1996 Everest climbing disaster.
   (A good follow-up to Krakauer's book is Beck Weathers' *Left for
   Dead*, 2000)

Ferd Mahler, *Under the Painted Eyes: A Story of Nepal*, 1999. Three short
   novels in one book, set in the shadow of the Himalayan Mountains
   and against the background of Nepal's fascinating history and rich
   culture.

Ella Maillart, *The Land of the Sherpas*, 1998. One of the first adventure
   books to focus specifically on the culture and domestic life of the
   Sherpa people.

Indra Majupuria, *Marriage Customs in Nepal*, 2009. An illustrated volume of traditions and marriage customs spanning various Nepalese
   ethnic groups.

Peter Matthiessen, *The Snow Leopard*, 1978. A haunting account of
   Matthiessen's amazing journey to the Inner Dolpo that became a
   classic Buddhist quest for inner peace.

Andrew Stevenson, *The Envelope: Walking Up to Everest Base Camp*,
   2009. Travel writer Stevenson walked nearly the same trek as we did
   on a pilgrimage to recover from the death of his brother.

About the Author

DAN SZCZESNY is a journalist and travel writer who lives in New Hampshire. His first book, *The Adventures of Buffalo and Tough Cookie*, is a hiking memoir about a one-year, 225-mile journey through some of New Hampshire's least known wilderness with his 10-year-old foster daughter.

Dan began his career in Buffalo, New York. Since then, he has written for a wide variety of regional and national publications, including the *Main Line Times*, *Philadelphia Weekly*, *Christian Science Monitor*, *Princeton Packet*, *Eastern Mountain Sports*, *The Good Men Project*, and *Pennsylvania Magazine*. In 2000, he moved to New Hampshire to cover the presidential election for the Associated Press. In 2001, Dan became associate publisher of *The Hippo*, the state's largest arts and entertainment journal.

He's a member of the Appalachian Mountain Club's 4,000-footer club and has written extensively about the outdoors and hiking. He has camped in the Grand Canyon and thru-hiked England's Coast to Coast Trail.

He lives in Manchester, New Hampshire with his wife Meenakshi. For more about Dan, visit www.danszczesny.com.

Life at the Top by Eric Pinder

Who would have guessed that the world's windiest, chilliest weather occurs not in the Himalayas but in New England? Indeed, New Hampshire's Mount Washington is known as "Home of the World's Worst Weather." We know the title is justified, because Mount Washington is also the home of a meteorological observatory, so we have the records to prove just how bad the weather is atop the "Rockpile."

A handful of hardy souls live at the Observatory year-round. Do they have to be just a bit unusual to seek out such a career? Perhaps. But the Observatory crew find much to enjoy in their icy home where they are also treated to spectacular sunsets, spine-tingling thunderstorms, and breathtaking toboggan runs.

In *Life at the Top*, Pinder describes with wry humor the joys and terrors of living in the clouds and explains Mount Washington's geology and weather. The last part of the book is a one-of-a-kind cookbook made up of recipes contributed by the Observatory staff—favorite dishes from people who take their meals seriously (especially in winter, when the food becomes spicier as the temperature grows colder).

Rime of the Ancient Underwriter by Jim Salmon

What's it really like to sail around the world on an old, square-rigged ship?

Jim Salmon found out when he quit his job as an insurance executive and signed onto a three-masted barque for a nineteen-month circumnavigation of the globe. *Rime of the Ancient Underwriter* is an account of his voyage of discovery aboard the *Picton Castle* out of Lunenburg, Nova Scotia. The world voyage was the subject of a popular, sixteen-part series on Canadian cable television called *Tall Ship Chronicles*.

Jim weathered storms at sea and stormy relations aboard ship, tramped through a steamy Panamanian jungle, climbed the rarified summit of Kilimanjaro, and tracked wildlife on the high plains of East Africa and the Australian Outback. There are pirates and a mutiny, but mostly his account is about people, places, and the human condition as seen through the eyes of a corporate exec turned seafarer.